WITHDRAWN

ABOUT THE AUTHOR . . .

Dr. Raymond W. McLaughlin has, since 1950, headed the Department of Homiletics and Speech at Conservative Baptist Seminary of Denver, Colorado. He has also taught in the same field at Denver University and Western Bible Institute. He has been visiting professor of semantics at Northern Arizona University, Flagstaff, Arizona, and visiting professor of Homiletics at Mission Mountain College, Polson, Montana.

Dr. McLaughlin earned his Ph.D., B.D., Th.M., and Th.D. at Northern Baptist Theological Seminary. In addition, he holds the M.A. degree from the University of Michigan and the Ph.D. degree from the University of Denver. He is a member of the Speech Association of America, The National Society for the Study of Communication and The Evangelical Theological Society. He has contributed articles to the *Seminary Study Series,* the *Seminary Biblical Study Series,* and to various periodicals.

COMMUNICATION
FOR THE
CHURCH

Dr. McLaughlin is one of the first scholars to bring power from modern communication theory and general semantics to the service of religion and church relationships. In this book he is providing very sharp tools to enable preachers and laymen to become aware of unconscious factors which make for misunderstanding, which block thinking, which interfere with listening in preacher-member, member-member, and intergroup associations. Most important, this book provides means to break through frozen attitudes, to release new and exciting meanings in religious symbolism and to help overcome confusions and misevaluations to which religious symbolism is prone. In this new orientation toward words which Dr. McLaughlin presents there may be carry-over into the entire life of the person who studies the book carefully.

ELWOOD MURRAY, PH.D.
Emeritus Professor and Director
School of Speech
University of Denver

COMMUNICATION
FOR THE
CHURCH

Raymond W. McLaughlin

ZONDERVAN PUBLISHING HOUSE
GRAND RAPIDS, MICHIGAN

To Alice
and the children,

Jan, Dan, Nan,
Dick, and Jim

With whom communication
is so easy

Introduction

One of the central problems of the Church is that of communicating the truth entrusted to it by its Lord. Therefore, it is important for Christians to be informed about advances in the comparatively new field of communication as a special discipline. Recent decades have seen the development of increased understanding of what communication is and how it is done. While the Church has always had some naturally gifted communicators within its membership, it needs help, especially during this time of kaleidoscopic change, in presenting the Gospel in our pluralistic American society. For it is possible for a Christian to hold a thoroughly evangelical theology and yet not have his witness listened to, let alone understood, because of inept presentation.

Related, as it is, to such disciplines as linguistics, semantics, psychology, and sociology, the field of communication now has its highly sophisticated aspect. But its principles are not beyond the comprehension of the layman in this area, provided that he has a competent guide.

Such a guide is Professor McLaughlin. With earned doctorates in both communication and theology, he has the added qualification of being a successful teacher. He writes with a refreshing avoidance of the specialist's jargon. But he does not over-simplify. Moreover, he constantly relates his discussion to the biblical evangelical faith and does this without lapsing into pietistic clichés. His book is a straightforward discussion of basic principles of communication as they relate to the work of the Church. Ministers, denominational executives, local church officers, Sunday school teachers, college and seminary students — in fact, all who are concerned with presenting the Christian message so that it will be understood — will find in Dr. McLaughlin's book an up-to-date and biblically oriented exposition of how to communicate the Gospel.

FRANK E. GAEBELEIN
Headmaster *Emeritus*, The Stony Brook School
Former Co-editor, *Christianity Today*

Arlington, Virginia

Preface

This book arises out of a conviction that Christians should and can communicate more effectively. A major problem with communication is that although everyone believes in it many are doing little about it. This is largely true because the communication process is complex and often misunderstood. Far too often communication is identified with the "stand up, speak up, and shut up" cliché, or with the questionable talent of flailing the obvious with three alliterative points. Effective communication goes much deeper than that. Understanding and a strong desire are the first steps in accomplishing communication. God's Spirit and love provide the power and means to carry it through.

This book is only a beginning, an introduction to Christian communication. It leaves much more to be said. There is always the *etc.* The rapidly changing universe will modify the conditions of human experience in a few years. Yet the basic notions set forth in the book are adjustable and should apply in the future as well as the present. Our task is to remain tractable, open to change, ready to adapt.

A deliberate attempt has been made to achieve simplicity and clarity so that laymen as well as students may read and understand the book. Communication principles need to be studied and utilized on a wide scale throughout the entire church. Accordingly, communication jargon has been kept at a minimum. It is hoped that contextual setting and definition will clarify meanings where technical terms had to be used. Readers deplore a communication book that does not communicate.

Students of communication will quickly recognize my dependence upon others in the field. I am indebted to writers in the fields of general semantics, group dynamics, and rhetoric for influencing much of my thinking. The footnotes and bibliography acquaint the reader with these and other sources which have helped me.

Several individuals have helped in the work and I want gratefully to acknowledge them. I express my deep appreciation to Dr. Elwood Murray, *Emeritus* Professor and Director of the School of Speech, University of Denver, and now Director of the Institute of General Semantics, Denver. Dr. Murray taught me, befriended me, inspired me, and constantly goaded me to write such a book as this. He read the manuscript and made valuable criticisms and suggestions. Dr. Frank E. Gaebelein, Headmaster *Emeritus* of the Stony Brook School, Long Island, New York and also formerly co-editor of *Christianity Today* read the material and made valuable criticisms and suggestions. In addition he graciously consented to write the introduction and helped in many other ways. I owe a special debt of thanks to Mrs. Dorothy Hampton of Denver, who painstakingly went over the manuscript and sharpened its style. Dr. Vernon Grounds, President, and Dr. Gordon Lewis, Professor of Theology at Conservative Baptist Theological Seminary, Denver, read the manuscript and made helpful criticisms and suggestions. The Rev. Dan Erwin, pastor of Bethany Baptist Church, Boulder, Colorado, arranged the index.

I am indebted to the members of the Zondervan staff for their interest and encouragement in the project over a sustained period of time. I wish to express my appreciation to the administration and board of trustees of the Conservative Baptist Theological Seminary of Denver for granting me a sabbatical leave so that I could finish a major part of the book. I owe a debt of thanks to Miss Marilyn Barrett for her help with many of the details of the work. And I am deeply grateful to my wife for her unceasing labor in typing the various editions of the manuscript.

Theologians and semanticists have sometimes seemed so far removed from one another in their thinking as to be virtually irreconcilable. My own conviction is that such an estrangement is not only unnecessary, but harmful. My hope is that there will be more cooperation between the two. Communication methodologists have much to offer to the church. The church has much to offer to communication. Both will profit when this is realized.

One of my former professors used to say, "The Bible is the greatest book ever written on communication." Christians applaud such a statement. Critics disagree. But my own continued study both of communication methodologies and the Bible forces me to agree with my professor. Communication methodologies provide the tools for communication, many of which can be seen in the Bible. And the Bible reveals God in Jesus Christ reconciling man to Himself and to one another. This book is sent forth with the prayer that all who read it will take up the tools of communication and with God's help will learn truly to share with Him and with one another.

RAYMOND W. McLAUGHLIN

Denver, Colorado

Contents

Chapter One

The Will to Communicate

COMMUNICATION IS THE SHARING of information for the purpose of affecting the receiver in some predetermined way. Communication may be verbal or nonverbal. Spoken or written messages, symbols, paintings, and music can all convey meaning.

Communication has purpose. The sender seeks to evoke a calculated response from his receiver. Some of the purposes of the communicator are understanding, stimulation, entertainment, and actuation. Teachers share knowledge with students in order to prepare them for living. Newspapers report facts but also mold public opinion. Stage plays, screen productions, and television programs entertain audiences and sometimes deal with public issues.

For Christians communication ought to be the sharing of information for the purpose of affecting receivers in some predetermined way consistent with the Christian Gospel and ethic.

17

Man's capacity for communication makes him unique. The physical scientist empirically demonstrates the differentiating characteristics of plant, animal, and human life. The psychologist explains to a certain degree the similarities and differences existing between the classes of life. The theologian insists upon the sensitive God-consciousness peculiar to human life. Virtually all agree that man's highly developed powers of communication set him off from the other classes of life on earth.

These unique powers enable man to formulate his evaluations of life into verbal and nonverbal symbols and thus to communicate. Professor Alfred Korzybski pointed out that because of man's singular capacity to symbolize he is able to profit from the fruitfulness of the labors of humans in the past, to share these advances in the present, and to contribute to that process wherein the past exists in the present, and the present will exist in the future. Man's ability to capitalize upon the time factor led to the label "time-binder."[1]

Contemporary communication clearly illustrates this time factor. Evolved from labors and findings of the past, it utilizes these discoveries in the present. It preserves these findings and contributes new ones for the future. The Christian church, too, has contributed greatly to the development of communication.[2] Few institutions utilize communication more than the church does today. And the future

---

[1] Alfred Korzybski, *Manhood of Humanity* (2nd edition; Lakeville, Connecticut: The International Non-Aristotelian Library Publishing Company, 1950), pp. 58 ff; also by Korzybski, *Time-Binding: The General Theory* (Lakeville, Connecticut: Institute of General Semantics, 1949); and Korzybski's *Science and Sanity: An Introduction to Non-Aristotelian Systems and General Semantics* (3rd edition; Lakeville, Connecticut: The International Non-Aristotelian Library Publishing Company, 1948), pp. 39, 183, *et passim*.

[2] The term "church" herein used refers to the universal church. The term "local church" refers to a local congregation of believers.

effectiveness of communication to Christendom remains to be seen.

Communication is important for many reasons. It is necessary for human function and survival. Business, pleasure, worship, and service would be impossible without the sharing of information. The world's vast economic structure would collapse without telephones, ticker tapes, cablegrams, and verbal and written orders. Social relationships would break down without discussion and reasoning. Without translations and instructions, the means for negotiations, statesmen would be baffled. Since we are social creatures, communication one with another is more important than we realize. Wars are won, liberty is preserved, and survival is enhanced by communication. Communication plays a vital role in earning money for life's necessities. It plays a vital role in negotiating for world peace.

The Christian outreach, no matter how noble, would be greatly hampered without sermons, books, or witnessing. Assistance to the poor, the suffering, the handicapped, and the oppressed depends upon communication. And in the sharing of the Christian message of faith, hope, and love to those who are lost it is no less important.

Communication is vital to the church because it is at the heart of Christianity. Just as life-giving medicine is useless unless shared with a dying man, so the Gospel is useless unless shared with the man who is lost. From its inception Christianity has embodied a message-sharing function. John the Baptist identified himself as "the voice of one crying in the wilderness . . ." (John 1:23). Jesus came preaching the Gospel of the Kingdom (Mark 1:14). Philip, quick to profit from his confrontation with Jesus, shared his newly found blessing with Nathanael (John 1:45). The early church though scattered by persecution, ". . . went everywhere preaching the word" (Acts 8:4).

For almost 2,000 years the Gospel has been shared by personal witness, corporate worship, fervent preaching, voluminous writing, and social activity. The church has seldom ignored advances in communication. First with the printing press, and then with radio, movies, and television, Christians have shared the truth of the Gospel. Now the Gospel can be broadcast to more souls by one program than the apostle Paul reached in his entire life. Today churches disseminate more Christian literature in one day than the Biblical writers turned out in fifteen centuries, even though qualitative differences are great. Pilots can fly missionaries half way around the world in less time than it would have taken Jesus to go from Jerusalem to Nazareth. If sharing is at the heart of Christianity, then communication is indeed vital, for communication is the instrument by which truth is shared.

The versatility of communication is important to the church. Language may be used for good or ill. It can be as effective in the spread of communism as it can be in the dissemination of the Gospel. Communication media are now equally available to dictators as well as presidents, to warmongers as well as peacemakers. Language itself either integrates or disintegrates peoples and nations. Words hurt or heal, inspire or discourage, enrage or pacify. They can condemn or liberate. The enslaving power of words can be great. The emancipating power of words can also be great if their function is understood. Therefore the church must turn communication's power and its versatility in wholesome directions, battling evil with good. The church must share the life-giving, mind-healing, soul-saving message of the Gospel with deceitful, rebellious, and self-centered persons who oppose it. World problems such as increasing nationalism, racial revolution, economic upheaval, and ideological conflict threaten humanity. The East and West have been likened to two scorpions imprisoned in a bottle. Each circles the other waiting to strike. Each fears to do so because this would trigger mutual destruction. The church suddenly faces an urgent challenge. It must work to prevent atomic annihilation and it must employ every available means of communication against disintegrative forces. Yet, before it can do so, the church of today must solve for itself one of the most baffling problems it has ever faced.

One of the most serious of problems confronting the church is its own communication breakdown. In this day when the most advanced technical and linguistic aids are immediately available, the church remains seriously entangled in its own communication lines. The church needs to ask itself a few probing questions. Why, despite the great amount of time given by the church to communication, is it not communicating better? Why, in spite of the great advances in electronic devices and linguistic techniques, are Christians still divided? Why, regardless of advanced education and improved communication media of all sorts, are Christians and religious denominations still plagued with suspicion, distrust, and sometimes open conflict?

Superficial answers to these questions are beginning to disappear. We now see that the mere possession of highly effective communication tools has not automatically produced effective communication. At the Paris Summit Conference of 1960 the most modern communication devices were employed to insure clear understanding. A speech delivered in Russian could be heard almost immediately in the language of the listener, due to brilliant translators with electronic instruments. Through radio, television, and newspapers the world within a few hours was informed of the latest proceedings. Yet little or no constructive communication took place, and the 1960 Summit Conference can be called one of the great communication blunders of our decade. Even the best technical devices and the most accurate reporting cannot guarantee communication of meaning.

Adolf Hitler showed us how easy it is for a person to talk peace and wage war at the same time. If this lack of a guarantee for the communication of meaning were confined to the non-church world, it would still be most serious. But such a communication breakdown in Christendom is perilous. The most obvious and most criticized example of this breakdown is church disunity. Some divisions may be justified, but splits on all levels of church life — universal, denominational, and local — have hurt the church's image.

Christianity needs to explore the possible communication breakdown in the increasing psychological problems of church members. 17,000,000 Americans, 1 in every 10, suffer from some kind of mental or emotional disorder and in the coming year approximately 300,000 people will become mental hospital patients for the first time. We are told that at one point or another many of these disturbed human beings turn to the church for help:

> Dr. Robert Felix, Director of the National Institute of Mental Health in the U.S. Public Health Service, has estimated that perhaps 40 per cent of the people take their personal problems first of all to ministers. The fact that so many people consult ministers speaks eloquently of the potential usefulness of this group in preventive and recuperative mental hygiene. The fact that so many people still need help *after* consulting a minister speaks with equal eloquence of the need for more adequate pastoral training in interpersonal relations.[3]

The upsurge in ministerial training for pastoral counseling, plus an ever increasing amount of literature on this subject, are signs of some progress in meeting the problems of interpersonal relationships in the church. A more thorough knowledge of the communication process will provide more help with these problems.

We need also to focus the church's attention upon other critical aspects of communication problems. The revival of interest in religion across America is encouraging, and

---

[3]Archibald F. Ward and Granville L. Jones, "Helping the Families of Our Mentally Sick," *Mental Hygiene*, XXXVIII (October, 1954), pp. 582-83.

every effort should be made to extend it. But the church, in spite of its attempted renewal, cannot overlook the moral and social evils existing within its midst. Christians may never succeed in closing the gap between theological belief and personal ethics, but they must keep trying. Modern trends have indicated anything but robust success with this effort. Gallup and Hill's survey of American youth discovered some discouraging religious discrepancies.[4] Large percentages expressed belief in such doctrines as God the omnipresent Judge, the reality of the hereafter, and the complete truth of the Bible. Yet in sharp contrast to these sterling beliefs these same young people lacked convictions on such things as rigged television quizzes and contestant bribery, cheating on examinations, or the reporting of dishonesty among fellow students. Similar inconsistencies have been uncovered among several groups of professing Christians.[5]

Equally serious spiritual problems compromise the church's social concern. It is difficult to explain the church's apathy toward the rise of militarism and the increase of secularism and materialism. Many wonder why the entrenchment of racial segregation in the United States exists in the Southern "Bible Belt" or why the eleven o'clock church hour on Sunday morning has been called the most segregated hour of the week. Concern on the part of many American Christians for destitute and hungry people around the world has dwindled.

The church needs to study more carefully the semantic problems that arise as it faces the increasingly difficult task of communicating the Gospel in language understandable

---

[4]George Gallup and Evan Hill, "Youth the Cool Generation," *The Saturday Evening Post*, CCXXXIV (December 23, 1961), 63-80.

[5]See "The Sad Case of Christian Morality," *Eternity*, XIV (April, 1963), 6-7; Paul Fromer, "On the Beach," *His*, XXIII (June, 1963), 1-4; 21-22; and Gordon H. Fraser, "A Survey of First-Term Missionary Casualties," *Bibliotheca Sacra*, CXV (January, 1958), 44-49.

to modern cultures at home and abroad. The Christian church lives in constant danger of becoming a middle-class ghetto shut off from society by personal aloofness and a private vocabulary. Rapid developments in education, science, and other fields threaten to make its ecclesiastical jargon obsolete.

Equally serious for the church is the problem of the distortion of information within its ranks. "Apostles of discord," as Ralph Lord Roy calls them, ". . . appear to be gaining in numbers and in strength."[6] All forms of false propaganda are being used by the unscrupulous to assassinate character, perpetrate falsehood, and breed distrust, conflict, and division. A form of religious "McCarthyism" has grown up which though frequently advanced in the name of Christ is hurting Christian testimony.

Communication may not be the panacea for all of the ecclesiastical ills described above. Nevertheless, it is difficult to imagine how the church should handle theological controversy, emotional imbalance, and spiritual and moral problems, without paying attention to the communication factors involved. The task of the church is a persuasive one. Therefore logical and semantic soundness is vital.

The church has refined its preaching through study of rhetoric. Now it must further clarify its language. Let every church member ask, "Why do Christians so often misunderstand each other?" "What linguistic barriers distort our witness to the world?" "What can I do to help?" Christians share information in many ways. They witness, conduct ceremonies, and display symbols. They write, read, talk, and listen. On the verbal level, Christians must speak and write clearly, responsibly, and authoritatively. On the nonverbal level, they must communicate an image which commands respect. Christians must merge their verbal and

---

[6]Ralph Lord Roy, *Apostles of Discord* (Boston: The Beacon Press, 1953), p. 3.

living images in such a way that any paradox which may seem to exist between the two is reduced to a minimum. As Christians labor toward this goal of reconciling lives with words, two factors ought to be kept in mind.(Controversy is as old as man himself and nothing is intrinsically wrong with it. Because it is so often embroiled in controversy the church is apt to develop a guilt complex. This may keep it from challenging the evils of society and human error. As the salt of the earth, Christians must be willing to endure misunderstanding, criticism, even persecution, if necessary.

Furthermore, Christians ought to recognize that communication breakdown in the church should lead to self-diagnosis and recovery. The church has not arrived at its goal. It continues to strive toward maturity. It takes seriously the challenge and testimony of the apostle Paul to the Philippians:

> Not as though I had already attained, either were already perfect: but I follow after, if that I may apprehend that for which also I am apprehended of Christ Jesus. Brethren, I count not myself to have apprehended: but this one thing I do, forgetting those things which are behind, and reaching forth unto those things which are before, I press toward the mark for the prize of the high calling of God in Christ Jesus (Philippians 3:12-14).

Christians can improve their communication. New tools for improvement stand ready. Those who desire may increase their knowledge of them. Skill in using them may be further developed. If we understand the communication process and are willing to use it, we can better understand each other.

Chapter Two

The Fundamentals of Communication

WE LIVE IN THREE DISTINCT yet overlapping "worlds." These are the worlds of experience; of evaluations; and of symbols, especially words. Put in the form of a triangle they look like this:

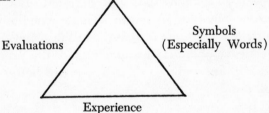

Notice the differences in these three worlds. The world of experience is made up of such things as objects, happenings, relationships, and emotions. It includes the body a man inhabits, the food he eats, the home he lives in, and

26

even the highway he uses. The stars overhead, the grass underfoot, the heat he feels, and the light waves he sees are part of this world. It is life and death, war and peace, love and marriage. This whole vast complex of relationships which a man can have on a nonverbal level of existence comprises the world of experience.

The world of evaluations is our mental world. Evaluation is our ability to understand what we experience, our capacity to put experiences together in a coherent whole. Judgment of what is good or bad is based on evaluations. These evaluations help us relate the events of the experiential world so that we either harm or help our fellowman. Evaluation is the time-binding capacity of humans, that capacity which is indispensable to the formulation of verbal symbols in the communication process.

The world of symbols is part of our world of communication. It may take two forms, nonverbal and verbal. The nonverbal is seen in such objects as crosses, flags, and emblems. Nature itself communicates on the nonverbal level as suggested by the psalmist when he wrote, "The heavens declare the glory of God; and the firmament sheweth his handywork" (Psalm 19:1). The world of symbols also includes written and spoken words. Language has become man's universal tool of communication. Words are the vital ingredient of prose and poetry. Through verbal and written communication man has the power to improve or impair society.

Relating the Three Worlds

Communication of truth takes place when these three worlds, experience, evaluations, and symbols, are properly related. From the speaker's point of view the communicative act shares symbolically life's experiences and evaluations. From the hearer's point of view the communicative act occurs when messages are accurately received and understood. When this process is successful people understand each other. But whenever the process fails, misunderstanding, confusion, distrust, and perhaps even conflict and tragedy may result.

If we are to communicate effectively, we must do our best to make our verbal maps fit the territories which they are intended to represent. A reliable road map of the United States must reproduce the layout, directions, and distances which exist in the nation's highway system. If the map does not correspond to the territory, it is not reliable and could lead to confusion or disaster. Reliability is always of utmost importance, even more so in case of crisis or national emergency.

Words, like maps, become reliable when they adequately express the experiences and evaluations they represent. When words do not accurately designate their referents, the likelihood of confusion, misunderstanding, and sometimes even danger exists. A misleading label on a bottle of poison could lead to tragedy. A left-turn sign placed at a point on a road which curves to the right could cause a fatal accident.

Men often place their trust in verbal evaluations of others. They trust in the verbal maps offered by doctors, lawyers, teachers, and ministers. They trust their physical being to the verbal advice of physicians and they heed the legal advice of attorneys. They place intellectual faith in the linguistic utterances of teachers and base spiritual faith on the accuracy of the Bible and on the counsel of clergy. The importance of making verbal maps fit their territories is obvious.

The historical successes and failures of Christianity attest to the necessity of verbal accuracy. Christians have spoken accurately enough to win one third of the world's population to at least a nominal belief in Christ. With words and deeds followers of Christ have preached the Gospel to the poor, have proclaimed release to the captives, have given hope to the handicapped, and have provided liberty for the oppressed. But by word and deed Christians have also alienated multitudes. Through inaccurate or distorted verbal communication they have misinformed and misled some. Individuals have been harmed and even destroyed. Churches have been disillusioned and divided. Clear communication of accurate statements does not always integrate people, but such clarity is almost always present where harmony and peace exist.

\Communication of the truth is essential to Christianity.(Misrepresentation, distortion, and carelessness with the truth can only sap the church of its spiritual strength. Christians must know and believe the promise of Christ, "And ye shall know the truth, and the truth shall make you free" (John 8:32). This truth then should be the object and essence of their messages. Every Christian's duty is to strive for accuracy in verbal communication. Communication of experiences and evaluations appears at first to be a simple process. It is not. Existing controversy, misunderstanding, and deception all testify to the difficulty of maintaining accurate verbal communication. Why is it so difficult to maintain? There are several reasons.

Sometimes men fail to make their words accurate because of carelessness. Some do not take time to check the facts of a story or an incident before they relate it. They may be careless because heavy obligations limit their time, or their carelessness may be part of their personality. Slovenly in dress, deportment, and intellect, these find the rigors of truth-finding and truth-telling tedious. In either case ethical obligations to society and to God demand some kind of adjustment.

Others fail to be accurate verbally because they are dishonest. Lying best fits their purposes. Language, because of its neutral character, provides them with a powerful tool for deception. Ways of distorting the truth are numerous and effective, and they may well become barriers to effective communication. For a dishonest man only the grace of God experienced through Jesus Christ can help.

The vast majority of people are not accurate verbally because they do not understand the complexity of the communication process. A superficial knowledge, or a hazy consciousness of the worlds of experience, evaluations, and symbols, leads them to equally superficial communication habits. Given a clearer understanding of these three worlds and their relationships, the average person can respond and improve.

I

THE WORLD OF EXPERIENCE

When we talk, we talk about objects, incidents, or feelings we have met in the world of experience. Our words are verbal sign-posts which point to events, and the subjects of our words exist on the experiential, nonverbal level of life. The problem plaguing the communicator is that of trying to make his words convey adequate information about experience. Words cannot take the place of human relationships or physical objects. How can words completely reflect the complex and subtle meanings of messages passed between international diplomats? Can words relate full information about the life-long devotion of a husband and wife, or of Christians laboring together in God's work? Do verbal symbols really portray the vastness of the Pacific Ocean or the rugged beauty of the rock-bound coast of Maine? Do verbal descriptions really communicate the sounds of a mountain stream cascading over boulders and plunging into deep pools? Words have difficulty conveying the smell of a pine forest or a trout frying over a camp fire. Robert Louis Stevenson said, "Language is but a poor bull's eye lantern wherewith to show off the vast cathedral of the world."[1] The infinite complexity of the experiential world defies complete linguistic description. Nevertheless we can and must share true information about it.

The Experiential World Includes the Physical World

The world around us is a physical world which we comprehend with our senses. Even to the most casual observer our physical environment possesses characteristics which render description difficult and thus complicates the problem of communication. Responsible communication must allow for the complexity of our physical world.

Continual process. One of the complicating aspects of our universe for the communicator is that of continual process. Heraclitus, the ancient Greek philosopher, claimed that a man could not step into the same river twice. This was true simply because both the man and the river were constantly changing. We speak of the "eternal hills," but even the mountains are continually eroding. Deep in the Rocky Mountains is the Mount of the Holy Cross. When the Mount was first photographed in 1873, the picture showed the cross cut sharply into the mountainside. The gleaming white cross slashed into a field of dark granite was visible for vast distances. But with the passing decades and the relentless storms the outline of the cross is rapidly fading away.

Continual process extends to other areas of existence. Ways of doing things change, and so do the people that do them. Governments and nations change. Who living at the time would have thought that the empires of Egypt, Babylon, or Rome would collapse?

Churches also change. Their architecture, modes of worship, methods of evangelism, and literature change. Their beliefs and their effectiveness change. It is a truism that

---

[1]Robert Louis Stevenson, *Familiar Studies of Men and Books* (London: Chatto and Windus, 1909), p. 67.

the church in 1968 is not the same as the church of A.D. 30 even though some insist on returning to the church of the New Testament. And pointedly, the church of 1968 is not the same as the church of 1948. The changes in the church in these two decades have been phenomenal, but we may find that the changes taking place during the next two decades surpass what took place in the entire last century. To overlook the dynamic changes which are taking place in Christendom today and to tell the world that this divine institution, the church, will always be the same is to mislead and to invite misunderstanding.

Theology changes. No one should ignore this, be he Christian or non-Christian; Catholic or Protestant; liberal or fundamentalist. No head-in-the-sand attitude can succeed even though the state of theological uncertainty may cause some to experience deep anxiety. Theological growth can be healthy and keep Christianity from degenerating into mere pharisaism.

Change can sometimes be harmful. But if we learn to condition our evaluations and attitudes toward such change, we will not be subject to delusion, deceit, or defeat. A wise person always allows for the possibility of the degeneration of interpersonal relationships. No rosy-tinted optimism which sees inevitable upward progress in man is justified. Emile Coue's philosophy of "Every day in every way we are getting better and better," was dealt such severe blows by two world wars that it is scarcely alive today. And we are becoming accustomed to living with the thought that at any time we and some of our philosophies could be destroyed in the mushrooming cloud of a nuclear explosion.

Since optimism regarding upward change in many situations is unjustified, careful observation and evaluation of the changing experiences of life applied to the church's manifold communication disturbances are mandatory. Only thus can spiritual health be restored. Theological flux, moral decline, psychological difficulties, and ecumenical efforts must be examined with realism.

By the same token, change may be beneficial. Mankind has suffered intolerably at the hands of stubborn people who have steadfastly resisted and even persecuted those more progressive or daring. One who experienced such opposition was Galileo. More than 400 years ago this brilliant astronomer and inventor contributed significantly to a new orientation toward life called "science" with empirical observation and experimental testing. But his theories and findings were ultimately challenged by powerful opposition, not the least of which was the fathers of the church. Subjected to inquisition and forbidden by the clergy to repeat his views, Galileo was forced to recant his convictions, though to have done so must have compromised his scientific soul. The ensuing years have changed this pattern. Today findings such as Galileo's are received and supported by pagan and Christian alike.

Certainly at the heart of the Gospel is the thrilling privilege of change. A man need not stay the way he is. If unregenerate men can radically change their lives, how much more can the regenerate? The Christian need not continue crying, "O wretched man that I am! Who shall deliver me from the body of this death?" (Romans 7:24). He may progress and say, "I thank God through Jesus Christ our Lord" (Romans 7:25). To one who has truly experienced the regenerative act through belief in Christ, the possibility of improvement within himself is surely obvious. No longer should a converted man say, "Once a failure always a failure; once a sinner, always a sinner."

One of the attitudes counselors frequently face in counselees is that of hopeless resignation. Individuals often tend to peg themselves on some level of former failure, seeing no hope of ever improving. The high-school graduate who earned poor grades may assume he will never be able to go on to college because he is a poor student. The business man who suffered bankruptcy may think himself always a poor risk. The girl who gave birth to a child out of wedlock may think she will always be marked as an evil woman. But knowledge of the regenerative power of the Gospel and consciousness of the inevitable law of continual process in life will help people to understand that no man need stay the way he is. The great potentialities of this profound truth are limitless.

How can we adjust our communication habits to provide for the law of continual process? In the first place we can adjust our thinking or evaluating to allow for it. We can train ourselves to reject the static attitudes perhaps ingrained in our minds. And we can reconcile our word patterns, our analyses, ourselves to provide for the constant changes we face in people, in situations, and in physical objects. We can develop a mind always ready for change. Secondly, we can adjust our language habits to reflect this constant change. Some form of what Alfred Korzybski designated as dating can be used.[2] We can condition ourselves to think and say that Germany of 1968 is not Germany of 1938, that John Jones of 1968 is not Johnnie Jones of 1945, or the church board of September 1968 is not the church board of March 1960. Though we cannot always be talking and writing in terms which have numerical postscripts, our language can reflect an attitude toward time and place which in turn indicates our consciousness of the reality of continual process.

Certain Continuities. In spite of the process character of our universe, certain continuities exist. Man changes but not completely. Churches are dynamic but thrive on certain

---

[2]Alfred Korzybski, *Science and Sanity: An Introduction to Non-Aristotelian Systems and General Semantics* (third edition; Lakeville, Connecticut: The International Non-Aristotelian Library Publishing Company, Distributed by The Institute of General Semantics 1933), p. xxxiii-iv.

traditions. Theology has its innovations but centers around the unchanging God.

Christianity teaches that eternal truth was revealed in the Bible. Christians take seriously the promise of Christ, "Heaven and earth shall pass away, but my words shall not pass away" (Matthew 24:35). And the words of the apostle Paul to the Corinthians recognize not just the transient, but also the permanent. "While we look not at the things which are seen but at the things which are not seen: for the things which are seen are temporal; but the things which are not seen are eternal" (II Corinthians 4:18).

Interpersonal relationships depend upon continuities. Although the Constitution of the United States provides for amendment, its strength lies also in its abiding laws. Education depends upon continuing principles as well as changing methods. Families find their stability in enduring love and loyalty.

Effective communication will reflect the abiding factors of life as well as the changing factors. Although we must state the old in terms of the new, we should not completely forsake the old. The Gospel, as old as Christ, and yet new, can be communicated in fresh and crisp terms. However, preoccupation with new expression should not lead one to jettison the eternal truths of the Gospel.

Limitless complexity. The nonverbal, physical world is characterized by limitless complexity. Non-identity, the fact that objects differ, is always present. No two objects are exactly alike in all respects. Natural things are all basically diverse and unique. The belief that twins can be identical is exploded under careful examination. No two identical snow flakes have ever been discovered. For the physical world is always dissimilar. This dissimilarity begins on the lowest level of structure, and from the submicroscopic level of atomic existence to the mammoth city skyscraper, diversity is always evident.

Yet human beings tend to place things together, ignoring the differences and magnifying the similarities. While a certain balance must be maintained between similarity and difference, we may fail to keep it. As a result we frequently catch ourselves calling all Jews greedy and all Negroes inferior. We find ourselves believing that all fundamentalists are ignorant, all liberals are skeptics, all Baptists are fighters, all Presbyterians are spiritually cold, and all churches are only interested in getting money.

The individual who is so preoccupied with similarities that he ignores differences tends constantly to oversimplify life. He develops what semanticists call the allness attitude toward existence. The allness attitude, permeating so many heated controversies in our day, uses the mechanism of identification as its tool. Identification is the mechanism of ignoring differences in objects and situations. It views all teachers, all religions, all marriage experiences as alike — as identical. In our church lives, the oversimplification of allness can harm us. When a popular magazine published an article several years ago which seemed to imply that "The Surprising Beliefs of Our Future Ministers"[3] were not only surprising but universally held by seminary students, a spate of heresy-hunting, charges and counter-charges was stirred up. A later article published by the same magazine put the situation on a much sounder basis by discussing "The Conflict Between Churchgoers and Their Ministers."[4] The later article revealed the allness attitudes of over-simplification and identification which permeated the thinking of many. Ministers frequently experienced frustration because ministerial and congregational values were not identical.[5] The truth is these values could never be identi-

---

[3]Jhan and June Robbins, "The Surprising Beliefs of Our Future Ministers," *Redbook Magazine*, CXVII (August, 1961), 36 ff.

[4]Ardis Whitman, "The Conflict Between Churchgoers and Their Ministers," *Redbook Magazine* CXX (January, 1963), 38 ff.

[5]*Ibid.*, p. 117.

cal. Ministers and congregations which allow for differences as well as similarities will avoid much controversy.

The woman who refuses to drink orange juice because as a child she was forced to drink it mixed with castor oil is oriented to allness, oversimplification, and identification. She identifies all orange juice with her unpleasant experience. The young minister who quit the ministry because his first church ignored his sense of values and convictions is guilty of allness, for he must not identify every church with the first.[6] And the individual who has had an unsatisfactory experience in a church must not forever leave all churches because of one incident.

The ignoring of complexity has another serious application. This is seen in the two-valued, either-or attitude which people develop. When this attitude is present an individual sees objects as either black or white, right or wrong, good or bad, for or against him. He ignores shades of gray which may include both sides. You are either for or against me; my friend or my enemy. One of Adolf Hitler's most vicious and frequently used tools of propaganda was that of the two-valued orientation, for in Nazi Germany one was either an Aryan or non-Aryan, automatically either a friend or a foe.

One of the great dangers of the modern ecumenical movement lies in the potentially two-valued nature of a large ecclesiastical institution. Churches are either in it or not in it. A unitary church must exercise every precaution to avoid discrimination against minority groups which refuse to join it. Church unity attained through intolerance and discrimination is disastrous. It has been in the past; it would be in the future. We must not allow our similarities to blind us to our differences in a race for unity at any price.

---

[6]Anonymous Clergyman, as told to Alfred Balk, "Why I Quit the Ministry," *Saturday Evening Post*, CCXXV (November 17, 1962), 32.

Frequent similarity. The nonverbal world shows not only complexity, diversity, and non-identity, but it also reveals certain similarities. While it is true that no two identical individuals have ever been discovered, there is a class of life called "man." Animals differ from trees, and insects from birds, but each has its generic and class similarities. No two Methodist churches are alike, but there is a Methodist denomination. Baptists may be of many varieties, but they do have some things in common.

Some men have fallen into difficulties because they have glorified differences and ignored similarities. In the early Christian centuries the Essenes became extinct because they separated themselves from normative Judaism and refused to marry and bear children. By exaggerating their differences through strict separation, the Essenes forsook the many similarities which they had with Jewish religion, and their sect ultimately disappeared. Exaggeration of differences can sometimes be as serious a hindrance as magnifying our similarities and neglecting our differences.

Because our physical world is characterized by both complexity and uniformity, our communication methodology must take these two factors into account. Evaluation and verbalization should reflect the many similarities and differences which exist. The necessity for such correct evaluation and verbalization to church life is obvious. In our intra-church and inter-church relationships we must avoid the results of either extreme identification or separatism, both equally harmful. Each church member cannot be poured into the same mold of rigid conformity. To go to the other extreme, however, and magnify differences so that we end up in completely separated cubicles within the church is just as harmful. If we magnify our differences out of all proportion to our similarities, we may become so separated that we fall into the danger against which Paul warned when he wrote, ". . . then you would need to go out of the world" (I Corinthians 5:10 RSV). Some groups are approaching such a state. On the other hand, to sweep aside our differences in a grand gesture of glorifying our similarities is to court comparable danger. There are contemporary groups which would belittle our differences in an all-out effort to establish organizational unity.

Effective intra-church and inter-church communication depends upon a balanced consideration of our similarities and differences. Both unity and diversity must be fostered. We must always remember the prayer of our Lord, "That they all may be one; as thou, Father, art in me, and I in thee, that they also may be one in us: that the world may believe that thou hast sent me" (John 17:21). We must also always remember those pointed words of Paul to the Romans, "For as we have many members in one body, and all members have not the same office: So we, being many, are one body in Christ, and every one members one of another" (Romans 12:4-5). In such a church body, similarities and differences, unity and diversity may function with effectiveness.

In order to adjust our evaluation and communication to this world of complexity as well as uniformity, we should think in terms of many values rather than just one or two. This allows us to be one or two-valued if necessary, but it also allows us to see many values in a situation if that is necessary. For example, we would be correct to say, as Socrates once said, "All men are mortal." We could also justifiably make certain two-valued statements such as "All men are either dead or alive." However, some situations in life are difficult to force into a one or two-valued mold. For example, psychiatrists sometimes find it difficult to decide whether a patient is sane or insane. They see degrees of both sanity and insanity in some patients. When is a man sick or well? Is a mulatto black or white?

The Bible is multi-valued. It makes certain one-valued claims, "For there is one God, and one mediator between God and men, the man Christ Jesus" (I Timothy 2:5); and again, "For all have sinned, and come short of the glory of God" (Romans 3:23). The Bible also makes some two-valued statements such as, "No man can serve two masters: for either he will hate the one, and love the other; or else he will hold to the one, and despise the other. Ye cannot serve God and mammon" (Matthew 6:24). Then, the Bible makes many multi-valued statements that must be interpreted in terms of degrees of more or less, such as, "For I say unto you, that except your righteousness shall exceed the righteousness of the scribes and pharisees, ye shall in no case enter into the kingdom of heaven" (Matthew 5:20).

Complexity and uniformity, similarities and differences, unity and diversity are best reflected in our evaluations and language by viewing life as having many values. Such a view of life allows the flexibility necessary to describe it accurately.

Relatedness. No object in our physical, nonverbal world stands in splendid isolation. Closely connected to the notion of similarities and differences described above, relatedness simply indicates that a person or an object exists in a field of intermeshing objects or personalities, and symbols. The communication process must provide for such relations.

Individualism is not eliminated in this view, but it is brought into proper relationship to the surrounding field. The communicator therefore becomes sensitive to others, their views, problems, limitations, values, virtues — feedback, in short, to their situation as a whole.

The Christian communicator holds that such sensitivity need not lead to hopeless relativity. The Christian is committed to God and His revelation through nature, Christ, and Scripture as changeless truth. God and His revelation are the points of reference through which linguistic descriptions of the experiential world, of which they are also a part, become meaningful. Otherwise everything, including this statement, becomes relative. The Christian position, however, does not eliminate all difference of opinion. The complexity of our universe, combined with our finite capacities of evaluation and communication, inevitably leads us to such differences. A consciousness of other points of view regarding belief in God and His revelation can aid us in our communication methods an'd help us establish more meaningful human relationships.

Therefore the Christian communicator must recognize relationships. He must realize that Christians may differently relate truths concerning God, Christ, the Bible, and nature. With a tolerant spirit and with a humble recognition of his own limited understanding and linguistic capacities, he should give himself to a study of God's total revelation. He should work for the establishment of God's will in the hearts of men, and he should communicate with care. He sees the truth in relationships but rejects crass relativism. Christians must insist that naturalistic relativism will lead to hopeless tension and ultimate despair. Carl Henry describes this condition, writing:

> The mind and will of man cannot rest in sheer relativism, yet its search of the horizons of only space-time process accommodates no absolute guides of conduct, nor workable rules with an imperative sanction. Naturalistic ethics moves within this distressing tension, disillusioning itself in romantic pretensions or yielding to nihilistic exhaustion.[7]

Knowing his interconnections with that larger reality of an absolute God and His revelation, the Christian has the orientation necessary for adequate communication.

Order. Our physical, nonverbal world is one of order. Order pertains to the big and little sequences, successions, regularities, arrangements, consecutivenesses, series, continuities, order of events in time, causes and consequences, cycles, rhythms, phases, antecedents, and outcomes.

---

[7] Carl F. H. Henry, *Christian Personal Ethics* (Grand Rapids, Michigan: Wm. B. Eerdmans Publishing Co., 1957), p. 91. Used by permission.

We see order in the sequences of solar activity such as day and night, in the seasonal manifestations of spring, summer, fall, and winter. We see order in the life cycle through conception, birth, growth, maturity, aging, and death. We see order in the very functions of man's physical body, and we see it in the phenomena of the total life processes and inter-personal relationships of human beings.

The underlying laws of order in our universe are at the basis of any intelligent reasoning, functioning, or communicating process. The communicator must determine the basic order and, to the best of his ability, form his evaluations and verbalizations to fit this order. Disobedience to the laws of order brings frustration and defeat. Alfred Korzybski argued that such attainments as intelligence, semantic reactions, survival, and orientation turn on the individual's adjustment to his own and the world's order and structure.[8] S. I. Hayakawa relates the human ability to integrate experience to our abilities of adequate symbolization and ordering.[9] Therefore adequate communication should adapt itself to the basic order of our physical and spiritual experience.

The Experiential World Includes the Spiritual World

We exist in a spiritual world as well as in a physical world. This spiritual world admittedly cannot be empirically demonstrated in the sense of scientific proof. God cannot be confined to the contents of a laboratory test tube. Human reason, however, must account for existence in some way or another. Gazing up at the stars a little boy asked his father, "Daddy, why was anything ever at all?" This simple question expresses the deepest searchings of the human heart and mind. We are faced with a final and profound

---

[8]Korzybski, *Science and Sanity, op. cit.,* p. 161, *et passim.*

[9]S. I. Hayakawa in consultation with Basil H. Pillard, *Language in Thought and Action* (New York: Harcourt Brace & Co., 1949), p. 154.

either-or choice. The two alternatives are a theistic world view or a non-theistic world view.

We choose between an intelligent purpose behind the universe or mere chance. The Christian finds it impossible to believe that the whole universe with its infinite complexity, continual process, differences, similarities, and relatedness could have happened by chance. The mathematical possibilities of such an accident defy rationality. A. Cressy Morrison, himself a scientist, former president of the New York Academy of Sciences, and author of the book *Man Does Not Stand Alone,* argued that our universe was designed and executed by "a great engineering intelligence." This assertion he based on what he called "unwavering mathematical law." He writes:

> Suppose you put ten pennies, marked from one to ten, into your pocket, and give them a good shuffle. Now try to take them out in sequence from one to ten, putting back the coin each time and shaking them all again. Mathematically we know that your chance of first drawing number one is one in ten; of drawing one and two in succession, one in 100; of drawing one, two, and three in succession, one in 1000, and so on; your chance of drawing them all, from number one to number ten in succession, would reach the unbelievable figure of one in ten billion.[10]

And the universe of which we are a part is so infinitely more complex a process than taking ten coins out of a man's pocket that to conceive of it as coming into existence and operating by chance is incredible. To believe the universe came about in such a haphazard way is like attributing the plays of Shakespeare or *Webster's Unabridged Dictionary* to an explosion in a printer's shop.[11]

The theist, in rejecting the idea of chance, does not

---

[10]A. Cressy Morrison, *Man Does Not Stand Alone* (Westwood, New Jersey: Fleming Revell Co., 1944), p. 13.

[11]Kurt Singer (comp.), "Nine Scientists Look at Religion," *Reader's Digest,* LXXXII (January, 1963), 92.

assert that the theistic view easily dissolves all problems. Nevertheless, in an effort to account for the mathematical precision of life in operation, the system of checks and balances in nature, and, above all, man himself with his spiritual, intellectual, and communicative potentialities — many thinkers adopt a theistic world view. Atheistic materialism appears to the Christian a grossly inadequate answer for such an intricate and rational universe. The Christian casts his lot with Sir James Jeans who concluded:

> Everything points with overwhelming force to a definite event, or series of events, of creation at some time or times, not infinitely remote. The Universe cannot have originated by chance out of its present ingredients, and neither can it have been always the same as now. For in either of these events no atoms would be left save such as are incapable of dissolving into radiation; there would be neither sunlight nor starlight but only a cool glow of radiation uniformly diffused through space. This is, indeed, so far as present-day science can see, the final end towards which all creation moves, and at which it must at long last arrive.[12]

The Christian's language should fit not only the territory of the physical universe, but also the spiritual territory.

II

The World of Evaluations

The importance of evaluation to the total communication task cannot be over-estimated. It is one thing to recognize the experiential and non-verbal world with its continual process, its similarities and differences, its relatedness, its order, and even its spiritual reality. It is another thing correctly to evaluate that nonverbal world. Many communication disturbances and breakdowns in the church and out of it can be attributed to poor evaluations.

---

[12]Sir J. H. Jeans, *Eos, or the Wider Aspects of Cosmogony* (London: Routledge and Kegan.Paul, Ltd., 1928), p. 55.

Why are poor evaluations so prevalent? They are prevalent because people often fail to understand the complexity of the evaluative process. Our waking day is spent observing life, making judgments, and talking about these judgments. This procedure has become such a habit that we consider it simple, take it for granted, and seldom give it critical thought. Evaluation proves to be a highly complex process made up of two activities which are influenced by a number of contributing factors. The two activities involved in evaluation are observation and judgment. The communicator should understand these two activities as well as the factors that influence them.

Observation

Although the ways of knowing are varied and helpful, the main point affecting communication is man's ability to observe what goes on about him. When related to the physical universe, this ability to observe depends mainly upon man's senses. Communication of sense data is affected by selectivity, variety, proximity, and change.

Selectivity. The physical experiences a man has depend upon which of his senses is stimulated. We know that a normal person can see, hear, touch, taste, and smell. Combinations of these sense experiences take place so that a man smells, touches, and tastes food almost simultaneously. Nevertheless, each of the senses is so differentiated that it responds to just one set of stimuli. Thus a colorful sunset is seen but not heard, felt, touched, or tasted. A sermon may stimulate the hearing and the sight but not the taste, touch, or smell. Our acquaintance with any event on the sense level depends upon which of our physical senses is activated. And because none of these senses is all-engaging, our acquaintance with any event will be specific and limited. As a result, our ability to communicate all of the factors about an event or an object is impossible. We must leave some details out because our senses did not impart them all to us. A realization that our evaluative and communicative ability is limited will help us see that we may not be perfectly understanding or understood.

Variety. The physical receptors of individuals show a wide variety of sensitivity to events and objects. A color-blind man views a painting differently than one who is not color-blind. A deaf person cannot appreciate the intricate details of a symphony. Certain afflictions may decrease one's sense of touch, taste, or smell. The addition of such factors as stimulation, fatigue, or intoxication affects one's sensitivity to life's experiences. Because of this variety of sensitivity in individuals, their acquaintance with objects and events becomes individualized and varied. All people do not see events in the same way. Difference of opinion is widespread. The Christian must be conscious of this complex situation and through love and patience adjust accordingly.

Proximity. Our physical position relative to an event or object affects our acquaintance with it. A player in a football game sees the game quite differently from a spectator. Similarly a church problem will be seen differently by the pastor and the people involved than by outside observers. The uncertain character of human observation is emphasized by proximity or lack of it. Under such conditions the communicator should recognize that no one can see all sides of an event or object at the same time. Adequate communication will mean that descriptions are modified in keeping with these limitations.

Change. The continual process character in life described earlier affects our evaluation of life. In the world of experience everything physical is subject to change. Ideas, individuals, and churches change either for good or for bad. The church's methods and interpersonal relationships have changed in such a way as to make observations of them virtually obsolete from generation to generation. The partial nature of our acquaintance with this vast and changing situation should dramatize our obligation to observe and talk about it with appropriate safeguards.

Judgment

Because our observations of life's facts are limited and individual, our judgments concerning them are limited. Man finds it impossible to view any event with absolute objectivity and completeness. As Paul once said, ". . . we know in part, and we prophesy in part" (I Corinthians 13:9). Recognizing that his knowledge is partial, the Christian must draw conclusions compatible with the evidence. His speech should let others know that he does not feel he has spoken the last word about things. The communicator should proceed to make value judgments in terms of the following criteria:

Knowledge. An individual's degree of general knowledge makes a difference in his value judgments. An American critic may have difficulty evaluating Chinese music, and a high-school student is scarcely fit to condemn the works of Michelangelo. A man with vast intellectual accomplishments will most certainly view an ecumenical council with more understanding than will another man with meager learning.

Specific knowledge of a given event will affect the value judgment of an individual immediately. A judge may be widely read on various aspects of the law, but unless he has heard the specific details of a case he cannot pass judgment upon it. An individual may be well versed in Bible knowledge but poorly fitted to counsel a couple about a marital problem because he lacks specific knowledge of the problem involved and of the field of counseling in general.

A communicator will certainly endeavor to broaden his general knowledge level and, before evaluating an event or person, obtain as much specific information as possible in order to base his conclusions on sound facts. The breadth and depth of one's knowledge, the extent of one's experience, and the variety of one's social and cultural background will profoundly affect the competence of judgment and communication.

Motivation. Value judgments are inevitably made in terms of one's motivation. Human beings go through life with basic physical and biological needs, including those of hunger, security, sleep, and sex expression. As an individual matures, he becomes aware of more complicated social and spiritual needs. Socially he becomes aware of the need for self realization, love, esteem, and group acceptance. Spiritually he becomes aware of such things as the need for worship, for reverence, and for repentance.

These needs, urges, or drives affect motives and emotional behavior. Pleasurable emotions such as love and joy are experienced when one's needs have been satisfied. Painful or distressing emotions such as anger, fear, or grief occur when satisfaction of one's needs is thwarted or threatened.

Human beings tend to arrange these various drives in some kind of hierarchy of preference. This hierarchy of preference does not remain unchanged but varies in terms of the circumstances at a given time. Thus, while a person's life may be oriented around a master motive of worship and Christian service, a great need for food or sleep could temporarily suspend the importance of the master motive. All value judgments are influenced by the priorities given one's needs, urges, and drives.

Value systems. Judgments based on observations are influenced by one's set of values. Even one's physical and social needs and wants are pursued in terms of a value system. Missionaries may suffer physical discomfort and personal deprivation because they consider their task of the evangelization of the pagan world to be of highest value in the sight of God. The best native hospital in the Congo is valuable to a medical missionary, but it might not seem as valuable to a medical researcher who would consider his cancer research laboratory in America more important. Both medical men may be dedicated Christians, but their evaluations may differ.

The Christian must recognize the complex character of the values held by himself and others if he is to make sound judgments. The vast number of religious, aesthetic, and political values often lead people to evaluate situations differently. Communication, therefore, depends upon one's patience and tolerance with those with whom he disagrees. The Christian set of values as given in the Bible must always set the limits of our evaluation and hence our communication.

Intensionality-extensionality. Judgments based on one's observations ultimately turn upon one's intensional-extensional orientation. The intensionally oriented person is one who depends upon words first and facts regarding the words later, if ever. The extensionally oriented person is one who tries to discover facts first and then considers words about these facts afterward. Obviously, no one can be either completely intensional or completely extensional. Neither extreme is desirable or even possible. However, sound judgments and effective communication will result more readily as one's outlook becomes more extensional.

Communication often breaks down between people who are satisfied merely with verbal descriptions unverified by facts. Gossip, hearsay, and libel thrive in such situations. People eagerly believe statements which appear in print or are carried by other mass communication media, and they do not bother to check factual bases. Effectiveness in both listening and speaking turns upon use of words based on facts. A double burden, therefore, falls upon each communicator. He must do his best to relate his judgments and words to verifiable facts.

The rapid progress of science is largely due to its extensional orientation. By its very nature science is more preoccupied with facts and objects than with words and descriptions. Religious groups tend toward intensionality and are thus frequently plagued by tensions, confusions, and divisions. Religion so often preoccupies itself with words and words about words that the facts behind these words grow dim or disappear. Such intensionality is not necessary. Though religion cannot be reduced to a physical science divorced from aesthetic values and moral judgments, the contemporary threat of world destruction demands that religious value judgments become more reliable and closer to the experiences they describe.

Evaluating Our Evaluations

The evaluative process in communication is complex. It is implemented by observation and judgment, and both are complicated by the controlling factors which operate in our physical and spiritual world.

Such complexity in the world of evaluations inevitably leads to varying points of view among individuals. Oversimplification of the evaluative process leads to disinterest in the differences which exist among people and thus to communication breakdown. Recognition of the complexity of the human evaluation process is an essential step toward human understanding. When understanding has been achieved, the third step in the communication process, that of putting our evaluations of the experiential world into meaningful language, can be taken.

III

THE WORLD OF WORDS

When we talk, we reduce our evaluations of the experiential world to verbal symbols. This verbalization is the third step in the communication process. We cannot forever remain in the silent worlds of experiences and evaluations. We must communicate with other human beings. Communication is predominantly verbal, reminding us that we live not only in the world of experiences and in the world of evaluations but also in the world of words.

Language is versatile. Words can help or hinder. Words can encourage, inspire, and reassure. But words can also deceive, enslave, and divide. Words have preserved the truth of the Gospel, the history of man, the law of the land, and the findings of science. But words have also contributed to wars, inquisitions, and purges.

Some communication is damaged through deliberate abuse of words. Hitler disrupted world communication through deliberate use of propaganda. Criminals consciously deceive others for personal gain or for self-protection. Communists have fomented dissension and social rebellion through the calculated use of words. Such tactics have caused widespread breakdown in human communication. More often, however, communication suffers because of failure to understand the nature and usage of words. On the individual level, the average person may unwittingly use such verbal distortions as overstatement and unfair labeling. These and other personal language abuses are far more subtle and widespread than the more spectacular tools of vicious propaganda. Yet in both cases, whether deliberately or unwittingly, words have been misused.

The understanding of the nature and function of words should help in the detection of verbal errors and avoidance or correction of such errors.

Words Are Not the Objects or Events They Describe

There is a difference between a word and its object. Though this simple principle called non-identity may at first appear to be glaringly obvious, it is fundamental to human understanding and its implications are far-reaching. Just as the word "steak" in itself is not the actual piece of meat which we eat, so the word "Christian" in itself is not actually that adult human being whose thinking has been oriented to a special type of life as embodied in Jesus Christ.

The word "war" in itself is not actually the total action in which men brutally destroy one another. The word "liberty" is different from its embodiment in various countries, and the term "equality" is not that complex set of interpersonal relationships which outlaws racial discrimination. There is always a difference between the word and its object or event.

Identification[13] of the word with its object or event may lead to confusion, misunderstanding, and even to delusion. Such extreme identification is seen in mental hospitals where patients sometimes identify themselves with someone like Christ or Napoleon. Identification may also be seen more commonly when superstition or word magic is practiced. Some hotels will not list a thirteenth floor because people refuse to stay on it. Some individuals will not voice the word "death" for fear it will occur.

Sometimes the identification of the word with the object can bring tragic results, as in the case of a suicide victim who had so identified himself with the label "failure" that he took his own life. No more fundamental principle of language exists than this one: the word is *not* the object or event it is being used to describe.

Words Are Abstracts of Their Objects or Events

Words are verbal or written symbols representing objects and events. They are language signs used to point to the

---

[13]Identification, as used here, means that words and objects are thought of as being the same. Non-identity means that words are thought of only as being labels of the objects they represent, and not part of them.

things they portray. Thus words, though telling something about their objects or events, never can tell all about them. Descriptive language always leaves out details.

This process of selectivity is known as the abstraction process. This abstraction process may be likened to picture-painting or map-making. Just as no picture or map ever yields all the details of its respective subject or territory, so no word ever conveys all the details of its referent. The word "man," though conveying a certain meaning, obviously fails to tell all about the complex physical, mental, and spiritual person-as-a-whole-in-action it is describing.

Different words reveal different levels of abstraction and of clarity. The words "utensil" and "knife" may both accurately describe a sharpened steel blade with an attached handle. The label "utensil," however, is more abstract, leaving more details out of its description, and it is therefore less clear in its meaning than the label "knife." The word "knife" is more definite, less abstract, conveying more details about its referent. Therefore the word "knife" is more descriptive than "utensil."

These different levels of abstraction may be applied to any object. At the top of page 54 is a chart showing the process of verbal abstraction using an apple as the descriptive object. It should be read from the bottom up. The chart illustrates certain conclusions about the abstraction process.

The levels of existence. In communication there are at least four levels of existence. (1) There is an objective level where objects exist as submicroscopic atoms and electrons in constant dynamic process. (2) There is an objective level where objects exist at the same time on a visible level which is recognizable, such as an apple, but not labeled with a word. (3) There is a descriptive level where objects are given a word label such as apple. (4) There are various inferential levels where objects are labeled with higher-order verbal abstractions such as produce, assets, or

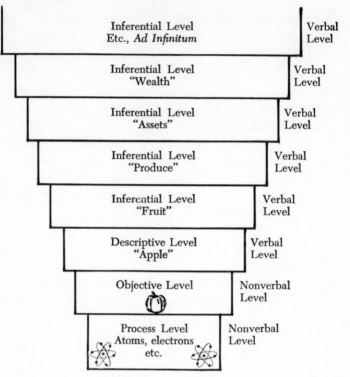

The Abstraction Process

The above chart illustrates certain conclusions about the abstraction process. (See page 53 for discussion of this process.)

wealth. These inferential levels of abstraction may go on indefinitely.

Abstractness and clarity. Higher level abstractions omit more characteristics about their objects than do lower level abstractions and thus tend to be less clear in meaning. Conversely, lower level abstractions convey more characteristics about their objects than do higher level abstractions and therefore are clearer in meaning. For example, the term wealth is much more vague and uncertain in meaning than the term apple. We may not know why a man is wealthy until someone tells us that he has made a fortune in apples.

Dead level abstracting. Talking on one level of abstraction is known as dead level abstracting. The most effective communication avoids this. Most minds find it difficult to follow speaking or writing which stays always on high level abstractions, but shallowness results when speakers and writers stay always on low levels of abstraction. The best communicators move up and down among the various levels of abstraction. They may state abstract principles and propositions, but they explain or apply them in concrete terms.

Abstracting and Self-Reflexiveness

Because language is abstract, it can be used to discuss itself. Words are used to discuss words. Newspaper editorials use words to evaluate the President's speeches. Men write verbal commentaries on the words of the Bible. Theologians debate the ancient creeds.

This verbal abstraction of verbalism is called self-reflexiveness. It is like the experience of walking into a hall of mirrors where we see ourselves reflected again, again, and again. Each succeeding reflection tends to be less clear until ultimately the reflected image may become blurred. So it is with the abstraction process. A statement cannot be the same as the statement it is describing. And statements about statements may become more abstract, more general, and hence less clear. Sometimes the basic image being discussed becomes blurred with the distorting reflections of language. Theologians would do well to remember the self-reflexiveness of linguistic abstraction when they argue over creeds which in themselves are abstractions of first-century persons and events. During the fourth and fifth centuries the church divided over the Christological controversies. Later, during the ninth century long and involved arguments between East and West developed over the meaning of the term *"filioque"* in one of the creedal statements. For this and other reasons, Roman Catholicism and Eastern Orthodoxy divided and remain so until this day. Awareness of the potential for misunderstanding in the abstraction process might do much to thwart controversy and division.

Words may have many Meanings

The abstract character of language means that words may have many meanings. The word "strike" may seem to be a simple word with obvious meaning. However, *Webster's Unabridged Dictionary* lists over eighty different shadings of meanings of "strike" in its verb and noun forms. The word "sin" occurs frequently in our English Bibles, but the ancient manuscripts reveal almost two dozen different Hebrew and Greek words with varied shades of meaning from which the English word "sin" is translated. Every language has many words of such plurality of meaning.

Because words have various meanings, they must be understood in terms of their contexts. Instead of wasting time insisting that a word must have one and only one meaning, it would be better to understand all words in terms of their contexts. Even dictionary definitions of words are based on contextual setting. Many a communication-destroying argument could be avoided if the debaters were aware of the multiordinality of language.

Words Are Communicative

Language conveys meaning in spite of its many complicating and limiting characteristics. The very elasticity of words is a major factor in our being able to communicate at all. Words often have to refer to different objects. Enough words to cover all the objects and incidents in our universe could not be manufactured, and figurative language would be eliminated.

Language communicates adequately for those who are aware of its limitations. We must·understand that we are always abstracting, that we are always leaving out some details of the discussion, and that therefore we may not be completely understood. When we are listening to someone else, the same principle holds true. His words are only abstractions of the total situation he is discussing, and therefore we may not be getting a clear picture.

The major method for clarifying words is that of modifying them in their contextual setting. Such modification may be carried out by various devices. Sometimes communicators close statements with "and so forth" in order to indicate that all has not been said about the subject being discussed. In writing, quotation marks can be used to show that the communicator is conscious of projecting a specialized meaning into a term. Contextual settings may be modified by the use of comparative terms, quantitative numerals, qualifying statements, and conditional remarks. Synonyms, similes, metaphors, analogies, and illustrations may clarify meanings. The complexity of the logical, grammatical, and rhetorical structure of language allows the meaning of a word to be modified in many other ways.

Religious Words are Communicative

Although most people agree that language is used meaningfully, many do not agree that religious language can be thus used. In recent years some semanticists and philosophers known as logical positivists have challenged the validity of metaphysical and theological discussions. These men contend that all knowledge of fact must be derived from sense experience. They also allow for statements expressing relations of ideas, but under close examination these statements turn out to be mere tautologies or arbitrary language conventions. Factually meaningful statements, according to positivists, must be verifiable by sense experience. The statement, "There are mountains in Colorado," is meaningful because it can be either affirmed or denied by a trip to Colorado. Thus statements that cannot be empirically confirmed are considered nonsense.[14]

The implications of logical positivism are widespread and dangerous, invading the most cherished areas of human life. According to it, statements about God, good and evil, justice, freedom, and eternal life are not true or false; they are nonsensical. This view makes truth relative and religious knowledge impossible. Only scientific knowledge can have factual meaning.

Two major objections have been raised to this radical philosophy. It is self-contradictory, and it leads to spiritual and moral bankruptcy.

In the first place, the self-contradiction of positivism weakens its claims. The basic proposition of positivism is that no statement of fact is meaningful unless it can be verified in sense experience. Such a claim may seem so obviously valid it warrants no contradiction. But, using their own criteria of judgment, we ask how positivists arrive at this truth. According to positivism's own avowed standards, only two kinds of statements make sense, logical statements and statements verifiable by the senses. However, the basic positivist proposition as stated does not fit either of the above categories. It is not regarded as a tautology, and it cannot be empirically demonstrated. The penetrating words of Will Herberg focus on this weakness of positivism:

> It is based on the premise that, aside from the rules of logic, only scientific statements, only statements of fact, have any meaning. This premise is a gratuitous assumption affirmed as dogma; it is, moreover, self-destructive. Not only does it sweep

---

[14]Nonsense as used here means not verifiable by our five senses.

away as so much nonsense virtually all human thinking — all, that is, but what has been devoted to logic and empirical science; in the end it turns upon and destroys itself. For the basic doctrine of positivism, as thus defined, is itself obviously neither a principle of logic nor the conclusion of an empirical science; it is, therefore, by its own criterion, nonsense.[15]

If logical positivism by its own standards can be proved nonsense, its threat is greatly weakened. Since it professes to operate by scientific criteria, it falls by its own hand.

In the second place, logical positivism is objectionable because it leads to spiritual and moral decadence. By ruling out of consideration whole areas of human experience such as the moral, and the religious, positivists violate the very scientific vows they espouse. To rule out these vital areas of human experience is to prejudge them in a most unscientific manner. Science is willing to accept evidence of all kinds without prejudgment. Right and wrong, love and hate, justice and injustice cannot be analyzed in a test tube. But their existence is nonetheless real, and these are the "nonsense" principles for which humans may fight and die.

The spiritual bankruptcy of positivists is seen in their contradictory treatment of value judgments. On the one hand, they claim that statements of value such as good or bad, better or worse, praise or blame are strictly expressions of private emotions. They are unrelated to the extensional world and are thus meaningless. On the other hand, they openly claim that their own positivistic methods are superior to other methods in spite of the fact that in so claiming they render the very kind of value judgments which they condemn as meaningless. The implications of this contradictory practice are freely admitted by one of their leading proponents, A. J. Ayer, when he writes:

---

[15]Will Herberg, *Judaism and Modern Man* (New York: Farrar, Straus & Giroux, Inc., 1951), p. 90.

> We feel that our own system of values is superior, and there-
> fore speak in such derogatory terms of his. But we cannot
> bring forward any arguments to show that our system is supe-
> rior. For our judgment that it is so is itself a judgment of
> value, and accordingly outside the scope of argument.[16]

Positivists thus greatly weaken their position by such self-contradictions. Their rigid scientific criteria rule out their own basic propositions. They pass value judgments in the very process of eliminating them. They ignore the differences between the nature of values and the nature of material objects, insisting that both be verified by the method of verifying the latter. And even though they urge the seeking benefit for all mankind, by their rigid criteria of verification they rule out of consideration those vital principles of human experience which men count most beneficial such as love, faith, and hope. Positivists are willing to trade beauty for ashes instead of ashes for beauty.

It is difficult to explain the great personalities of history in terms of such spiritual, intellectual, and moral poverty. Can one explain Jesus Christ in terms of such poverty? Did not St. Paul, Luther, Judson and Livingstone give themselves to those qualities and principles of human experience that positivists relegate to the realm of emotional nonsense? Indeed they did. They are superb examples of those to whom life's spiritual, moral, and aesthetic principles were just as real as material objects and much more vital.

Few thinkers want to throw out the advantages of the scientific method. Verification of one's thoughts and words as far as possible is not only commendable but necessary for effective communication. The insistence upon referring one's assertions back to the objects they represent is of utmost importance. But experience must be interpreted to in-

---

[16]From *Language, Truth and Logic* by Alfred Jules Ayer (New York: Dover Publications Inc., n.d.), p. 111. Reprinted through permission of the publisher.

clude spiritual, intellectual, and moral realities as well as those material objects verifiable only by the senses.

One must constantly check his words against the sense experience of the physical world, but more than that, against the moral experience of the spiritual world. The vast findings of modern science guide us in the realm of the physical. The voluminous contributions of the Judeo-Christian tradition guide us in the spiritual realm. There is much more to discover in both, and both are necessary for an adequate approach to modern communication.

Summary

We live in three distinct yet overlapping worlds. They are the world of experience, the world of evaluations, and the world of symbols, especially words.

Communication takes place when these three worlds are properly related. From the speaker's point of view the communicative act involves seeing life's experiences, evaluating them, and describing them. From the hearer's point of view the communicative act occurs when he receives messages and understands them with relative accuracy.

Communication is often hampered because people oversimplify the process of relating these three highly complex worlds. Nevertheless in spite of their complexities they can be related, and communication can take place. However, the most effective communication will take place only as those communicating are aware of the capacities and limitations of language.

Chapter Three

The Process of Communication

COMMUNICATION IS A PROCESS, not just an act. It is a process because the language used, the object described, the participant involved, and the event itself constantly change. And communication is a circular process, moving from sender to receiver back to sender, and so on. Clear understanding of this process depends upon knowing something about its types, its levels, and its ingredients.

I

THE TYPES OF COMMUNICATION

There are three types of human communication. They are frequently labeled intrapersonal, interpersonal, and group communication. Christians add another, spiritual communication, and it is most important. Spiritual communication links man to God through prayer and the reading of God's Word. It also links man to man through the sharing of God's love.

Intrapersonal Communication

A human being carries on extensive communication within himself. Through reflection, inner argumentation, and other intellectual exercises we send and receive many messages that do not get outside our own bodies. Intrapersonal communication is, of course, the primary and foundation step toward subsequent interpersonal and group communication. Without intrapersonal communication, there could be no further steps. Intrapersonal communication has three basic functions — evaluation, resolution, and adjustment.

Evaluation. As described in Chapter Two, evaluation involves observation and judgment. In intrapersonal communication one observes the physical and spiritual events of human experience, weighs them in his thinking, and makes judgments on them. Because human beings are finite and because the universe of experience is complex, one soon discovers that there are limitations to his evaluative capacities. Accordingly he adopts an open-minded approach to evaluation. The open-minded approach to evaluation does not excuse one from decision-making, but it does reserve for him the right to consider new evidence and adjust to it.

Evaluative tangles, blockages, and errors are many. They may be psychological, calling for professional counseling. On the other hand, they may be intellectual, calling for straight thinking. Or they may be spiritual, in which case counsel with a competent minister will help. The importance of the evaluative function in man's inner communication depends upon the mind's intellectual capacities, but unless these capacities operate with adequate psychological, logical, and spiritual health, their usefulness will be limited.

Resolution. The evaluation of life's experiences seldom is an end in itself. The human mind makes decisions, agreements, or resolutions from it. One may procrastinate, but that in itself is a decision. Resolution is at the heart of morality and spirituality. A person makes resolutions with himself to carry out any action. Fulfilling resolutions with himself and others contributes to healthy intrapersonal communication. Breaking resolutions with himself and others endangers the inner communication system. The major threat to keeping one's inner agreements is ego-centricity. This threat is manifested in such sub-threats as rationalization, procrastination, and making exceptions of oneself.

These tricks of self-deceit can be ruinous. Our intrapersonal communication centers can become so tangled as to be useless. One cannot communicate with others if he cannot communicate with himself. Paul, realizing this truth, said to the Corinthians:

> Every athlete exercises self-control in all things. They do it to receive a perishable wreath, but we an imperishable. Well, I do not run aimlessly, I do not box as one beating the air; but I pommel my body and subdue it lest after preaching to others I myself should be disqualified (I Cor. 9:25-27 RSV).

And Jesus was even more piercing in His Sermon on the Mount saying:

> Why do you see the speck that is in your brother's eye, but do not notice the log that is in your own eye? Or how can you say to your brother, "Let me take the speck out of your eye," when there is the log in your own eye? You hypocrite, first take the log out of your own eye, and then you will see clearly to take the speck out of your brother's eye (Matt. 7:3-5 RSV).

Our duty as Christians is clear. The path of righteousness and integrity is before us. To refuse to travel it will not only sabotage our intrapersonal communication systems but will involve us in sin. James very clearly points out, "Whoever knows what is right to do and fails to do it, for him it is sin" (James 4:17 RSV).

Adjustment. Evaluation and resolution must be subject to constant adjustment in intrapersonal communication. However, self-correction of errors is extremely difficult, if not impossible, because of one's high degree of subjectivity and low degree of objectivity. Professional counselors have recognized the need for comparison of the self with some outside person in order to help a person see his own errors.

Theologically, Christianity has always stressed the inability of man radically to change his persistent egocentricity. Christ saw this human predicament and, while talking to Nicodemus, the Pharisee, declared ". . . Truly, truly, I say to you, unless one is born anew, he cannot see the kingdom of God" (John 3:3 RSV). Christianity therefore teaches that nothing short of a spiritual rebirth will help a man in the correction of his inner errors. Christ becomes the "other person" with whom the Christian compares his own life. For after this spiritual rebirth evaluation, resolution, and adjustment will be viewed in terms of Christocentricity rather than egocentricity.

Evaluation, resolution, and adjustment are the never-ending functions of intrapersonal communication. The more adequately they function, the better will be one's mental, and spiritual health. Once this health is attained, individuals are prepared for effective interpersonal communication.

Interpersonal Communication

Communication between two people is called interpersonal communication. Insertion of a second person into the communication process complicates it. Both participants must understand that gaining complete information about each other's messages is impossible. No two people will ever completely understand each other. However, adequate understanding is possible and communication can be satisfactory as long as both persons recognize that a margin of misunderstanding may exist.

Interpersonal communication may suffer if either or both participants inject unacceptable moral, emotional, or cultural factors. Anger, authoritarianism, or ignorance creates barriers to successful understanding.

Interpersonal communication is enhanced and meaning clarified by metacommunicative factors. Metacommunicative factors are such things as expressions, gestures, body posture and tension, and even tone of voice. By use of these, the very important factor of attitudes is communicated.

The correction of errors in messages is greatly facilitated by the presence of two participants. With two people present, facts may be challenged, explanations and defenses may be introduced; and comparative evaluations, resolutions, and adjustments are possible.

The use of two participants calls for potential equality of responsibility for effective communication. Unfortunately there is a widespread idea that if people are not listening to a preacher, politician, or some other type of communicator, the fault always lies with the communicator. Contemporary findings in the field of listening and comprehension challenge this assumption. Today many communication methodologists suggest that responsibility for effective communication must be as much the listener's as it is the speaker's.

Group Communication

Many people assume that human relationships develop arithmetically — that is, the introduction of each new member to a group simply adds one more relationship. In reality, human relationships do not develop arithmetically, but geometrically — that is, the introduction of each new member to a group means the introduction of a whole new set of relationships. Compare the following tables: Arithmetical Progress: 2, 4, 6, 8, 10, 12, 14, 16, 18, etc. Geometrical Progress: 2, 4, 8, 16, 32, 64, 128, 256, 512, etc.

The student of communication should quickly realize how human relations and associated problems tend to mushroom as one moves from intrapersonal and interpersonal to group communication. The multitude of problems accompanying increase in group numbers should be considered seriously by local churches that are intent upon building huge and unwieldy memberships. Large memberships have obvious advantages in terms of financial strength and community image, but the corresponding loss of communicativeness is cause for grave concern. Jurgen Ruesch and Gregory Bateson warn of this predicament: ". . . completeness of information obtained by any given individual in an organized group decreases with every increase in complexity and differentiation of the system."[1]

If the major task of the church is communication, then the church should resist every barrier to its effectiveness. Bigness can defeat Christians in their most important task.

II

THE LEVELS OF COMMUNICATION

Turning to the personal element in the communication process, we note that a further complicating factor is present. Communication takes place on not one but two levels.

The Nonverbal Level of Communication

Frequently people think of communication as being only verbal, whether in written or spoken symbols. However, there is a type of communication that cannot be reduced

---

[1] Jurgen Ruesch and Gregory Bateson, *Communication The Social Matrix of Psychiatry* (New York: W. W. Norton & Company, Inc., 1951), p. 281.

to words, for it is nonverbal/ This nonverbal communication has been called metacommunication or communication about communication.[2] \A man does not simply speak; he speaks in a certain way, attitude, /or spirit. /His very presence and appearance say something not confined to his words./ Love may be communicated between two people simply by a meaningful glance, a smile, or a touch of the hand. Disapproval may be communicated by a frown or a threatening gesture.

Nonverbal communication is especially important to the Christian community. Non-Christians usually respond more readily to Christian action than to Christian verbalism. An unethical life often cancels a Christian testimony. Also, \nonverbal communication extends beyond a man's character to include his attitudes and even his appearance./ These silent factors communicate in a powerful way. They may communicate positively or negatively depending upon their function in the life of the speaker. Accordingly, the Christian ought to be aware of the nature and function of metacommunication.

The Verbal Level of Communication

Important as they are, the nonverbal factors are not enough. The communicator must ultimately move to the verbal level. Words are tools for the impartation of ideas. Many complicated and extended ideas cannot be communicated by silent level pantomime or nonverbal symbolic demonstration. They must be handled verbally.

Verbal communication skills may be developed in many directions. Speakers may improve their vocal and bodily factors in the delivery of messages. They may study and work on rhetorical factors, and they may improve their conversation, discussion, and counseling techniques.

---

[2]*Ibid.*, pp. 23-24.

The communicator's facility in verbal communication is closely related to his understanding and use of the semantic triangle discussed in Chapter Two. He will be the most effective when he communicates his evaluations of human experience with accuracy and skill.

Verbal and nonverbal factors in the communication process may be seen in any live speech situation involving the communicator, the receiver, and a message. Let us now examine these ingredients.

III

The Ingredients of Communication

The types and levels of communication point us to the ingredients involved in the communication process. At this point it is necessary to broaden the scope of the process beyond the semantic triangle discussed in the previous chapter. Experiences, evaluations, and language must be placed into their total context of operation.

A number of communication models have been suggested through the years. The ingredients range from Aristotle's simple threefold classification of speaker, speech, and audience[3] to the more technical factors of the Shannon-Weaver model which includes a source, a transmitter, a signal, a receiver, and a destination.[4] For present purposes the process of communication will be viewed as involving four major ingredients — the communicator, the message, the channel, and the receiver. Technical refinements and additions to this model are, of course, necessary and will be

---

[3]Lane Cooper (trans.), *The Rhetoric of Aristotle* (New York: D. Appleton-Century Company, 1932).

[4]Claude Shannon and Warren Weaver, *The Mathematical Theory of Communication* (Urbana: The University of Illinois Press, 1949), p. 5.

discussed, but in general any communication success or failure can be traced back to one of these factors.

Remember in this connection that the speech process is seldom, if ever, a strictly one-way affair. It does not simply proceed from speaker to listener and then stop. Communication normally moves in a circular movement. Note the following example.

An idea forms in a communicator's mind. The mind transforms this idea into verbal symbols. The communicator's nervous system activates his vocal apparatus which in turn transforms the verbal symbols into audible speech. The speech sounds are carried over wave patterns in the air and ultimately fall onto the listener's ear drums. The speech sounds then travel over the listener's nervous system to his brain. Here the sounds are decoded into meaningful verbal symbols, and the listener reacts to the communicator by vocal or facial expressions. The communicator senses the listener's reactions and adapts his continuing messages to influence further the listener until the initial purpose is fulfilled or defeated. Here the speaker is the communicator, the organized ideas are the message, the words are carried as sound over the channel of the air waves (telephone, radio, television, newspaper, or other instruments could serve as additional channels), and the listener is the receiver.

The chances for a possible communication breakdown in this process are many. Poor evaluation, wrong assumptions, inadequate word choice, distracting noise, jammed channels, poor hearing, wrong interpretation of ideas, personal bias, negative feedback, and many other possibly complicating factors may cause the communication to fail. For each of the four ingredients, the communicator, the message, the channel, and the receiver, is vital in the success or failure of the communication process.

A

The Communicator

Traditionally, the greatest single force in communication has been the communicator, especially his *ethos,* or intrinsic character. Aristotle contended that the character of the speaker was the most vital of all the means of persuasion:

> It is not true, as some writers on the art maintain, that the probity of the speaker contributes nothing to his persuasiveness; on the contrary we might almost affirm that his character (*ethos*) is the most potent of all the means of persuasion.[5]

However, the effectiveness of the communicator extends beyond character and includes speaking skills. Quintilian, a Roman teacher of rhetoric in the first century, became famous for his definition of the ideal communicator:

> My aim, then, is the education of the perfect orator. The first essential for such an one is that he should be a good man, and consequently we demand of him not merely the possession of exceptional gifts of speech, but of all the excellences of character as well.[6]

Two major factors, then, figure in the effectiveness of the communicator — character and skills. In a sense character and skills are roughly analogous to the nonverbal and verbal levels of communication. Note the various factors involving the communicator which contribute to effective communication.

The character of the communicator. Character is built upon certain personal qualities, for both character and reputation are vital to the communicator. Character can be distinguished from reputation because reputation is what people think about a person while character is what the person really is. An individual must seek to develop those

---

[5]Cooper, *The Rhetoric of Aristotle, op. cit.,* p. 9.
[6]H. E. Butler (trans.), *The Institutio Oratoria of Quintilian* (Cambridge, Massachusetts: Harvard University Press, 1953), I, 9.

qualities of character which will establish the highest reputation. The qualities of integrity and morality communicate favorably to others. Dishonesty and immorality communicate unfavorably to others. If the highest moral standards are demanded of secular communicators, how much
more ought they to characterize Christian communicators!
Moral loftiness gave a powerful impetus to the speaking of
the prophets, Jesus Christ, and the apostles. In the secular
world similar oratorical power was attained by men like
Abraham Lincoln and Winston Churchill.

The qualities of open-mindedness and fairness communicate favorably to others, whereas the qualities of stubbornness and bigotry communicate adversely to others. The
open-minded man is oriented to the attitude of "non-allness."
He resists the role of the know-it-all. His fairness is revealed
in his willingness to listen to others' ideas, arguments, and
problems. Few communication-destroyers are as effective
as stubbornness, closed-mindedness, and bigotry.

The quality of selflessness as opposed to selfishness is
considered another strong contributor to effective communication. A self-centered person can repel others, while
a selfless person often attracts. The essence of Christianity
lies in its power to shift a person's center of devotion
from self to God and to others. It was our Lord Jesus
Christ who in answer to the scribes' question about the
great commandment, said:

> . . . Thou shalt love the Lord thy God with all thy heart, and
> with all thy soul, and with all thy mind. This is the first and
> great commandment. And the second is like unto it, Thou
> shalt love thy neighbour as thyself (Matthew 22:37-39).

The quality of courage in one's convictions communicates favorably. Suppression of facts to protect one's self
communicates negatively. Courage of conviction is not stubbornness and bigotry, but an intrepidity born of deep-

seated persuasion that the truth for which one speaks brooks no compromise and that it must be stated.

The supreme quality of character for the Christian communicator is spiritual maturity as opposed to immaturity and carnality, or fleshliness. Spiritual immaturity and fleshliness in the lives of Christians can be seen at the heart of many church problems. Theological controversies, church splits, interpersonal tensions, and individual selfishness are loaded with such immaturity. The great giants of the faith throughout history have inevitably revealed a high level of spiritual maturity and sensitivity. Paul, Luther, Edwards, and Truett, to say nothing of a great host of other Christians whose names will never be known world-wide, were effective through the spiritual maturity of their lives. The apostle Paul compares and contrasts these two diametrically opposite types of life in his letter to the Galatians when he writes:

> But I say, walk by the Spirit, and do not gratify the desires of the flesh. For the desires of the flesh are against the Spirit, and the desires of the Spirit are against the flesh; for these are opposed to each other, to prevent you from doing what you would. But if you are led by the Spirit you are not under the law. Now the works of the flesh are plain: immorality, impurity, licentiousness, idolatry, sorcery, enmity, strife, jealousy, anger, selfishness, dissension, party spirit, envy, drunkenness, carousing, and the like. I warn you, as I warned you before, that those who do such things shall not inherit the kingdom of God. But the fruit of the Spirit is love, joy, peace, patience, kindness, goodness, faithfulness, gentleness, self-control; against such there is no law. And those who belong to Christ Jesus have crucified the flesh with its passions and desires. If we live by the Spirit, let us walk by the Spirit. Let us have no self-conceit, no provoking of one another, no envy of one another (Galatians 5:16-26, RSV).

The communicative power of each of these two types of life, the spiritual and the fleshly, is apparent. Living the life of spiritual maturity will aid the Christian cause beyond calculation.

The attitudes of the communicator. Attitudes are part of a communicator's *ethos* or character, and are important enough to study in terms of their applications. Such attitudes as honesty, impartiality, sympathy, sincerity, and sensitivity have vital implications for the communicator as they are directed toward himself, toward his subject, and toward his listeners.

The powerful and effective communicator who is honest with *himself* recognizes his strengths and limitations. He reveals confidence and poise, controls his emotions, acts with humility and modesty, and carefully prepares his messages. In contrast, the audacious communicator who delights in defiance and bigotry, who is inconsistent, who derides the need of preparation, and demonstrates lack of discipline, is apt to communicate negatively.

The communicator who views his *subject* with seriousness is apt to be effective. Listeners frequently are able to sense lack of preparation, flippancy, fanatical bias, and disregard of facts on the part of speakers. Careful attention must be given to the material, arrangement, style, and presentation of messages whether delivered to small groups or large audiences.

The communicator's attitude toward his *listeners* is important. Now and then there are persons and audiences whose masochistic nature allows them to enjoy abuse and domination, but such are the exceptions, not the rule. Most listeners want to be treated with sincerity and impartiality, with respect and love. Listeners will seldom object to rebuke or correction if given in the spirit of fairness and love. Most listeners rebel, at least inwardly, against being browbeaten or denigrated. The communicator should not fawn on his listeners but should treat them with sincerity and respect.

The appearance of the communicator. The physical appearance of a speaker, though a silent factor, is eloquent. This silent eloquence extends to one's natural mien — one's height, weight, and general appearance. Physical attraction and appealing personality seem always to give advantage to their possessors. Upon seeing Daniel Webster, the great American orator, walk by one day, an observer is reported to have said, "Nobody can be as important as Daniel Webster looks." Webster's ability certainly extended beyond his appearance, but his dignity and impressive bearing were so great that he was often called the "godlike Daniel."[7]

A communicator's assumed appearance — his carriage, poise, dress, forcefulness, and sincerity — contribute to his effectiveness. Men like John F. Kennedy in the area of politics, Douglas MacArthur in the area of the military, and Billy Graham in the area of religion have all shown those dynamic qualities of vitality, assurance, and commitment to their causes which have strongly contributed to their communicative ability.

Self-discipline, proper restraint, and a controlled temper contribute to the communicator's effectiveness. Although we respond favorably to a speaker who does not spare himself in animation and force, we withdraw from one who loses control of his temper or emotions. The display of strong emotion in speaking is generally thought to be not only acceptable but necessary. For example, how else can we treat the great Christian themes of love, sacrifice, and salvation, except with deep emotion? But deep emotion does not necessarily imply weeping or other excessive displays. At this point self-discipline and proper restraint are imperative.

The communicative power of a speaker's appearance also extends to certain personality traits, such as eccentricity and uniqueness. The employment of characteristic symbols

---

[7]Robert Irving Fulton and Thomas Clarkson Trueblood, *British and American Eloquence* (Ann Arbor, Michigan: George Wahr Publisher, 1912), p. 225.

also has its effect. Billy Sunday was known for his colorful antics, his flamboyant gymnastics in the pulpit. Billy Graham is known for his unique repetition of the phrase, "The Bible says." Many speakers have become known in terms of the symbols associated with them — Winston Churchill for a stubby cigar protruding from his mouth, and John F. Kennedy for the shock of thick hair that hung over his forehead. Sometimes delight in the use of symbols communicates negatively. The blatant parading of swastikas and then the hammer and sickle became repulsive during the era of the Third Reich. Much care must be taken in the conscious or even unconscious use of personal eccentricities and symbols.

The knowledge possessed by the communicator. A speaker's words frequently reveal his level of knowledge. Listeners may quickly sense the breadth and depth of his observation, his experience, and his academic background. Formal education and private study can help a communicator widen his acquaintance with the sense experience of the physical and intellectual world and with the moral experience of the spiritual world. Lacking in extensive knowledge, the communicator sharply curtails his effectiveness. Cicero felt that orators ought to know virtually everything:

> In my opinion, indeed, no man can be an orator possessed of every praiseworthy accomplishment, unless he has attained the knowledge of everything important, and of all the liberal arts, for his language must be ornate and copious from knowledge, since, unless there be beneath the surface matter understood and felt by the speaker, oratory becomes an empty and almost puerile flow of words.[8]

A communicator's effectiveness also depends upon the thoroughness of his knowledge of the specific subject he is discussing. Theological seminaries can train a minister in methods of research, but only a minister's personal integrity

---

[8]J. S. Watson (trans.), *Cicero on Oratory and Orators* (Philadelphia: David McKay, Publishers, 1897), p. 17.

can drive him to thorough preparation before preaching on a given subject. Churches need to develop more lay-leadership training courses to help their teachers and officers in the demanding task of lesson preparation for Sunday school. Careful expansion of church libraries and encouragement of members in wide reading will ultimately increase the churches' communicative powers.

The evaluations of the communicator. A speaker's words reveal not only his knowledge but also his evaluative ability. His powers of observation and judgments of value may remain hidden until put into words. Keenness of observation may be developed through an understanding of the nature of sense perception. A constant awareness that acquaintance with objects is at best limited will protect the speaker from over-statement and should keep discussions open for the reception of further evidence.

The communicator's words are the keys to understanding his set of values. His messages tell us something of his emotional maturity, his cultural interests, and his intensional-extensional orientation. Value judgments are based on all of these factors.

The detection of bias in a communicator is not as important as the discernment of his particular kind of bias. No one is completely extensional or objective. Although complete objectivity is desirable, it is more elusive than many realize. In 1938 Franklin Delano Roosevelt made the shrewd observation,

> To be objective is an achievement. We are born with emotions, and we easily acquire prejudices. It is natural to coddle, pamper, and nurse them until they turn on us and boss us, and lash us into a daily shriek. To see the facts through this haze of emotion, to let them filter through, to keep still and let the facts do the talking — that, if you've never tried it, is an achievement.[9]

---

[9]Franklin Delano Roosevelt, "Trademarks of Quality," *Chicago Daily Times*, November 29, 1938, p. 17.

The communicator, whatever the difficulties, should try to move constantly toward greater objectivity. An objective viewpoint will aid him in making sound value judgments. The more objective the speaker, the more apt we are to accept his conclusions. Such objectivity and the resulting acceptance are important to the successful communicator.

The communication skills of the communicator. A knowledge of communication and skill in using it are vitally important to the communicator. It is true, of course, that men untrained in the methods of speaking and writing have occasionally been successful communicators. Most of these, however, are quick to admit that they would profit by greater understanding of the communication process. The person who takes the pains to study to improve his knowledge of communication will discover that knowing how consistently to develop good communication is infinitely superior to stumbling occasionally upon a successful message.

There are four basic communication skills — speaking, writing, reading, and listening. After extensive research, Dr. Paul T. Rankin of Ohio State University found that the average American spends 70 per cent of his waking day in such verbal communication. Of this verbal communication day he discovered that we spend 45 per cent of our time listening, 30 per cent speaking, 16 per cent reading, and 9 per cent writing.[10]

Speaking and writing skills may be developed by private reading or formal class work. Voluminous writings are available in all fields such as rhetoric, homiletics, semantics, journalism, and creative writing. Formal education in these fields may be pursued to the doctorate level. Some may not need such training. However, most people have insuf-

---

[10]Paul T. Rankin, "The Importance of Listening Ability," *English Journal,* College Edition, XVII (October, 1928), 623-30.

ficient natural ability along these lines and will therefore profit by further training.

Reading speed and comprehension can be developed by private effort or by formal course work. Literature and technical aids are available in either case. Listening skill is important enough to demand special attention and will be considered more carefully in connection with the communication receiver.

These communication skills for the writer extend to the choice of subjects, invention, and arrangement of material, and stylistic excellence. For the speaker, all of the skills needed for a writer plus personality, vocal, and bodily factors influence the communication impact. Excellence in the communication skills means excellence in the communication process.

Ancient and modern writers agree that the communicator's character and communication skills are powerful factors in communication. The ideal communicator has both in balance. Communication skills, of course, may be used with telling effect by demagogues. History has illustrated that. But the influence of demagogues has been short-lived and history also records their disasters. Character is the essence of Christian communication as well as the repudiation of demagoguery. Thus, while communication may always remain a powerful tool in the hands of unethical people, the Christian communicator must add character to communication skills, confident that righteousness will ultimately prevail over unrighteousness.

B

The Message

The nature and function of the message in the communication process can vary with purpose or interest. Our approach to the message in communication is that of *fidelity*. As high fidelity in the electronic world refers to faithfulness in the reproduction of sound, so that term will be used to refer to the faithfulness of messages to their objects. Other highly developed approaches to the study of messages are grammatical and syntactical make-up, linguistic characteristics, logical coherence, and rhetorical factors. All of these factors bear upon and contribute to the logical, semantic, and persuasive soundness of communication. However, we are primarily interested in message maps that reveal high fidelity to the territories they represent.

High fidelity in messages depends upon four interconnected ideas or notions. These notions are elements, structure, order, and relations. And understanding of the meaning and application of these notions will work toward fidelity in communication.

The Meaning of Elements, Structure, Order, and Relations

Each of these terms is a high-order abstraction. Each is multiordinal; that is, each has different meanings depending upon its context. The interrelation of the four notions makes a definition of each difficult because their similarities may obscure their differences. Yet for clarity and understanding a general and non-technical definition of each is important.

Elements. This notion refers to the basic parts, the simplest components, the fundamental rudiments of any object, person, or event known to man. For example, a house is made up of such elements as bricks, wood, and nails. These elements are the things men talk about.

Structure. This idea refers to the pattern of arrangement of interdependent elements. Even if bricks, wood, and nails are elements of a house, they are not a house until they are put into that kind of a structure. The same elements could be arranged in the structure of a church or of a school.

Order. The term order as used here refers to the arrangement or sequence of objects or events in time and space. For example, our physical universe goes through a certain sequence of seasons in order. Life follows a cycle of conception, development, birth, growth, maturity, aging, and death.

Relations. The connection between objects, persons, and events is their relations. Nothing exists by itself. Every element, person, event, or idea is dependent upon some other element, person, event or idea. Knowledge is not knowledge of isolated objects or things, but of their relationship to something else. Try to conceive of gold as a completely isolated element. Such conception is impossible. Even the mental image is related to such things as color, weight, and substance. Whatever exists for man has relations.

The Application of Elements, Structure, Order, and Relations

The communicator should develop a consciousness of the applicability of the four notions as defined above to our physical, spiritual, and linguistic worlds.

The physical world. Everything in our physical universe has elements, structure, order, and relations. Physical scientists work constantly to discover these four in various things. The phenomenal advances of modern science are built upon the proper understanding and utilization of such information. Take man himself, for example. Medical scientists have been able to improve immeasurably man's life by getting to know him better. They study his physical elements; his basic structure; the order of his physical, nervous, and mental functions; and his relationships with his total environment. No one can completely comprehend our complex universe in terms of these four characteristics, but the more we know about them the better we will be able to communicate.

The spiritual world. Obviously the elements, structure, order, and relations of the spiritual world are more difficult to discern and to agree upon than those of the physical world. However, the difficulty involved becomes part of the challenge. The Christian sees the four factors in a Biblically oriented life. The elements are God, Christ, man, revelation, salvation, and so on. The structure is the whole complex body of Christian theology. The order may take various forms such as creation, fall, redemption, and consummation. The relations may be complex and varied but would certainly involve God's relationship to man, man's relationship to God, to himself, and to other men. The Christian communicator faces a life-time task of studying the nature and function of physical and spiritual existence in order to help him communicate adequately.

The linguistic world. Language has its own elements, structure, order, relations. The basic elements of language are aural and visual symbols — we call them sounds and letters. These sounds and letters are meaningless until structured in some order which by previous agreement is significant. When properly related to other sounds or letters and to the objects they seek to describe, they take on meaning. For example, take the elemental letters *hcrhuc*. The linguistic elements or letters needed to describe some object are there. Yet the reader does not know what the elements mean because as yet they have no meaningful structure, order, or relationship. The elements rearranged in terms of their structure, order and relations read *church* — a verbal symbol having a realistic referent.

In the linguistic world as in the physical and spiritual worlds these four notions apply on many levels of abstraction. Thus elements, structure, order, and relations in language extend to words, phrases, sentences and so on. Messages involve content, grammar, style, logic, and other complex factors. Their fidelity to the levels of existence now becomes paramount.

Working Toward High Fidelity of the Message

High fidelity in a message occurs when the elements, structure, order and relations of the words of the message correspond with the elements, structure, order, and relation of the objects, events, or persons they are describing. In order to be accurate and dependable, the verbal map must fit the described territory.

Attainment of high fidelity in messages is not easy. The communicator must keep working toward it. Although the complexity of our physical and spiritual worlds plus the abstractness of language make *complete* fidelity impossible, adequate correspondence of words to objects is possible and such correspondence is adequate for effective communication.

The content of messages, of course, is greatly dependent upon all of the grammatical, logical, and rhetorical factors of communication. The effective communicator must find adequate content for his messages. Then he must try to present that content with the greatest effectiveness. Only then will messages be significant.

During World War II a question was printed over the desks of many London broadcasters who were beaming daily messages to enemy countries. This question was, "Is what you are saying worth a man's risking his life to hear?"[11] Such a question is appropriate to every Christian. Is the message we are communicating worth a man's giving his life to hear?

C

The Channel

The third ingredient in the communication process is the channel through which messages are sent. Communicators

---

[11]Halford E. Luccock, *Communicating the Gospel* (New York: Harper & Brothers, 1954), p. 42.

use the term in various ways such as physical, technical, mass, and group channels.

Physical Channels

Sometimes message channels are discussed both in terms of the speaking apparatus or the motor skills of speakers and in terms of the receiving apparatus or the sensory skills of receivers. Efficient communication obviously depends upon the condition of this equipment and accompanying skills in usage. In most cases these motor and sensory skills can be improved. Speaking and listening, for example, can be improved by training. Even some physical defects in these mechanisms can be alleviated by medical treatment. Where training or correction will enhance communication effectiveness, they should be utilized.

Technical Channels

Technical scientists view communication channels in such terms as light waves and sound waves. Some adjustment of these channels is possible through such means as room arrangement, acoustical improvement, the use of public address systems and better lighting. Because this is usually the field in which engineers work, communicators should utilize them wherever improvement is needed.

Mass Channels

Christians have found powerful channels in the mass media — radio, television, newspapers, magazines, and films. If the reaching of the masses is the communicator's object, then he ought to keep several considerations in mind. He must decide on the best medium in terms of what he can afford and what he is able to produce. Television poses problems in both of these areas. Few churches or individuals can afford the high costs of television time, and fewer are equipped to produce the kind of programs that compel popular attention. The results are twofold. Christian communicators too often settle for television's off-hours and then produce the kind of a traditional church service that unchurched people avoid in the first place.

Radio time does not normally pose as great a financial problem as television. However, the level of many Christian radio programs still leaves much to be desired. This means that Christian radio programs frequently end up being heard by the churched while the unchurched remain unreached. Here again, isolated radio stations, off-hours, and poor programming should be avoided if radio communication is to be effective.

Christian writing for publication has proven to be an increasingly successful venture. Christians are better trained, are writing to meet more relevant needs, and are succeeding in reaching more non-Christians than ever before. Nevertheless, Christian writers still face the major problem of reaching the unchurched. Christian publications are effectively serving the Christian population, but their impact upon non-Christians is limited. If Christian writers can get their messages launched through channels which reach the unconverted, they will have scored a major triumph. The quality of Christian writing will determine its chances of acceptance in such channels in the future.[12]

Group Channels

Strong channels of communication exist within groups. These channels may be very complex and subtle depending upon the size and organization of the group. In rather

---

[12]On mass communication see such works as John W. Bachman, *The Church in the World of Radio-Television* (New York: Association Press, 1960); Malcolm Boyd, *Crisis in Communication* (Garden City, New York: Doubleday & Company, Inc., 1957); and Malcolm Boyd, *Christ and Celebrity Gods The Church in Mass Culture* (Greenwich, Connecticut: The Seabury Press, 1958).

highly structured groups such as most churches, position status, office, and other such designations of relationship are very important. These relationships determine the nature of the communication channels within the group.

Basically, communication within the group moves in two directions — vertically and horizontally. Vertical communication moves up and down between leaders and followers. Horizontal communication moves back and forth between individuals on the same level. Direct and indirect communication takes place within and between these levels.

If a group is complex, several or many levels of office, status, and role may exist. In a corporation, for example, one frequently sees a president or chairman heading a series of vice presidents who in turn preside over a number of junior executives who run a staff of workers. Most churches operate on such a structure. If the church is large, it may have a pastor who, sometimes with one or more associates or assistant pastors, presides over departmental superintendents who supervise teachers who then work with the total membership. Boards and committees function within the entire organization. In such a structure intermediary personnel usually communicate both vertically and horizontally. They engage in upward communication with higher-level officials, in downward communication with lower-level officials, and in horizontal communications with equals.

Group channels of communication should have two major characteristics. They should be open channels, and they should be used in proper ways.

Open channels of communication should be maintained between all levels and individuals within the group. Leaders ask for trouble when they ignore chances for response or otherwise allow channels to become clogged. An unhealthy group is one in which the interpersonal channels of group communication are clogged, and a healthy group is one in which these channels are open.

Personal observation, to say nothing of technical research,

has discovered that trouble may arise when proper channels of communication are not used. A communicator may cause resentment or even open hostility by shortcutting or by-passing an immediate superior in order to hasten a decision or action from a higher-up. Following normal channels of procedure may take longer but may build better interpersonal relations. Christians would do well to study the vast complex of group relationships as they bear upon the channels of communication within the local church.

Which Channel Will Be Used?

Channels of communication are important to the Christian mainly in terms of what he wants to accomplish. Normally, little attention is paid to them. However, widespread developments in the fields of visual aids and mass communication media coupled with new knowledge of individual and group communication behavior demand that more careful attention be given to these channels. The wise communicator will analyze his communication purpose and send his messages over the most effective channel or channels.

Use of more than one channel is often advisable. If the communicator can reach the receiver by way of sight or touch in addition to hearing, chances of understanding are vastly improved. Use of visual aids is becoming more popular not only among teachers but also public speakers. Use of objects that can be felt or even tasted may convey powerful meanings.

The church's use of mass media is still somewhat limited. These channels should be increasingly used in the future.

D

The Receiver

The receiver or auditor is the fourth factor in the communication process. We have stated that the receiver also acts as a communicator through some type of feedback and the communicator, sensing this feedback, becomes a receiver. An overlapping in nature and function is therefore present. The similarities and differences between the receiver and communicator are important to the understanding of the communication process.

The Personal Characteristics of the Receiver

The receiver, like the sender, has an ethical image (*ethos*) which includes certain characteristics.

The character of the receiver. The receiver's ethical and moral character will affect his reception of messages. The qualities of integrity, impartiality, and spiritual maturity will determine the kind of listening and consequent response the listener will give to the communicator.

The attitudes of the receiver. The listener's attitudes toward himself, the subject being discussed, and the communicator will affect his reception of and action on the speaker's messages. Confidence in one's own critical powers, open-mindedness toward the subject being discussed, and fairness and courtesy toward the communicator can make the difference between a mature listener and a gullible one.

The appearance of the receiver. The receiver's appearance can and usually does affect the communication. Alert bodily and facial expressions denoting attentive interest in a speaker's message create a type of response to which the communicator will respond favorably and will adjust his material accordingly. Boredom, disagreement, or even disgust are also clearly communicated to a speaker. Even a receiver's dress, whether neat or slovenly, can either communicate respect or discourtesy to a speaker.

The knowledge of the receiver. Breadth of knowledge and experience affect the reception of messages. Although such knowledge and experience in the receiver may be more silent than spoken, they depend always upon an understanding of words. Most scholars agree that thought requires mental symbols, but they do not always agree on the nature of the symbols. Pictorial, verbal, and even imageless theories have been advanced. However, many if not most of our thought units are language units, and the limits of our language may at least partially determine our perception. Therefore the broader a man's knowledge and experience, the broader his understanding of messages will be.

The evaluation of the receiver. The evaluative ability of the receiver affects his reception of messages. A listener's powers of observation and soundness of judgment will determine the nature of his response. Keenness of sense perception, physical distance from a communicator, and clear understanding of the message will play an important part in the receiver's function. One's emotional maturity, his values system, and his intensional-extensional orientation will modify his part as a receiver in the communication process.

The communication skills of the receiver

The communication skills possessed by the receiver are vital. Strictly speaking the receiver is either a reader or a listener. In either case, however, the more he knows about the total communication process, the better able he will be to read or listen. At this point the receiver, like the communicator, would profit by knowledge in such fields as rhetoric, homiletics, and semantics. Such knowledge though certainly profitable is not mandatory, however, to successful reception of messages.

The receiver as a reader. If the receiver is reading, he can improve his speed and comprehension. Contrary to popular opinion increase in reading speed can bring increase in comprehension. Moreover, improvement in reading skills is not always dependent upon youth or intellectual status. Poor reading habits are not inborn; they are acquired. Researchers have discovered certain habits which are hindrances to effective reading. These hindrances are seeing individual letters instead of whole words; subvocalizing — that is, subconsciously sounding each word as one reads it; reading one word at a time instead of phrases or groups; regressing — that is, going back over what has already been read; poor concentration; and reading everything at the same speed. Some readers even add such mechanical hindrances as tracing with the finger, underlining with a pencil, or sliding down the page with a ruler. The elimination of such hindrances will increase reading speed and comprehension. Home study courses as well as formal college classes are available to the individual who wishes to improve his reading skills.

The receiver as a listener. The receiver usually functions as a listener. Research evidence indicates that people spend about three times as much time listening as they do reading. This seems to be true in spite of the fact that emphasis in our schools in the past has been just about the opposite to these findings. Only recently have communication specialists begun to emphasize that the listener is at least as important as the speaker in the communication process.

Thus a major factor of listening has to do with its *importance.* In spite of the fact that listening occupies three times as much of our communication time as does reading, many people dislike the discipline attentive listening demands. It is puzzling and sad to realize how many listeners can and do avoid listening to a good sermon, let alone a poor one, by never attending church. And most of us are aware of many conversations in which we have been personally involved when we or the other conversationalist were listening with a vacant stare and a disengaged mind.

One of the benefits of keen and alert listening is that good listening contributes to good speaking. Any communicator, whether a preacher, a group participant, or a conversationalist, will respond favorably to an attentive listener, speaking at his utmost effectiveness.

Good listening significantly contributes to knowledge. Aside from the sense of sight, the sense of hearing is the greatest channel of human learning. In addition to facts gained, good listening may teach us much language facility and about facets of human behavior. Listening allows one to observe some metacommunicative factors present in a spoken speech but absent in a written message.

Perhaps listening is most important for the Christian because of its therapeutic value. Listening is mutually good therapy for the listener as well as for the speaker. Perhaps that is why Paul urged the Galatian Christians to "Bear one another's burdens, and so fulfill the law of Christ" (Galatians 6:2, rsv). A good listener experiences personal benefit when he realizes that he has helped someone else by listening to him. The therapy a listener provides to another individual who must unload or unburden his mind is well known to pastors and counselors.

A second major factor of listening has to do with our *preparation* for it. We listen for three basic reasons in addition to the therapeutic purpose. We listen for enjoyment, for information, and for inspiration. If we are going to profit from an approaching listening experience, we should make some advance preparations.

We need to be mentally and emotionally ready to listen. Good listening takes great energy and can be a demanding experience. As a good speaker progresses toward a climax in his speech, audiences tend to become tense, to concentrate, straining for every word. Without this rapt attention, this expenditure of energy, the listener will not respond properly, the speaker may flounder, and the whole communication experience may fail. Poor mental attitudes and emotional blocks may ruin the all-important rapport between speaker and receiver or receivers.

We need to prepare ourselves physically for listening, for physical conditions may often be barriers to effective listening. Physical factors fall into two categories, the personal and the environmental. Personal physical handicaps are such things as fatigue, discomfort, or hearing difficulty. Poor ventilation, being too far from the speaker, distracting noises, and inadequate lighting are examples of environmental barriers.

We need to prepare ourselves intellectually for listening. Wide reading and experience challenge the mind and make it appreciative of a wide range of ideas. Specific reading and experience on a subject being discussed equip an auditor to listen both intelligently and critically. It stands to reason that a listener who is well read in the field of theology will better understand a lecture on contemporary theological problems than a listener who has done no reading in the field.

A recognition of the difference between thinking speed and talking speed is also part of the intellectual preparation for good listening. The human mind thinks with tremendous speed. Speech moves at a relatively slow rate. An American's average speaking rate is approximately 125 words per minute, whereas our span of absolute attention has been found to be only a few seconds.[13] Consequently when we listen to someone talk, we listen in spurts. Our attention functions something like alternating current in electricity. Between the word and thought groups of the speaker we may agree, disagree, anticipate, or evaluate. And in addition to these lightning-like activities, we allow our minds to wander to other thoughts. We may remember an appointment made for next week, our child's cold, or

---

[13]See W. B. Pillsbury, *Attention* (New York: The Macmillan Company, 1908), Jon Eisenson, *The Psychology of Speech* (New York: F. S. Crofts & Co., 1938); and M. Billings, "Duration of Attention," *Psychological Review* XXI (1914), 124-135.

our golf game of yesterday. Only as we thrust aside intruding thoughts and discipline ourselves to sew together as many of the speaker's word and thought groups as possible will we understand him accurately. A consciousness of the fact that thought speed is so much greater than speech speed should help us prepare to listen.

A third major factor in listening has to do with *methods.* Some ways of listening are better than others. We can listen without any purpose or effect, or we can listen with definite purpose and plans. In the first place we should listen intelligently. Speeches will generally be formal or informal. If we are listening to a formal speech, certain rhetorical clues will contribute to our understanding. The speech will have three general parts — an introduction, a body, and a conclusion. The speaker may start his introduction with an attention-getting illustration, quotation, or statement. Soon after that he will state the central idea of his message in the form of a basic proposition, or thesis. This basic proposition is one of the most crucial parts of the speech, and the listener should be awaiting it. The rest of the speech will be a development of this proposition, perhaps an explanation or form of argumentation.

Once the listener has discovered the basic proposition, he should study the proof or elaboration of it in the body of the speech. Each major point in the body of the speech will be a sub-proposition, supporting the main theme. These sub-propositions in turn will be established by such rhetorical processes as narration, interpretation, illustration, application, argumentation, and exhortation. The conclusion may briefly summarize the proposition and main points of proof or explanation, and then bring the central idea of the speech to a climax by means of a vivid illustration, an apt quotation, or a bit of telling poetry. Although all speeches do not follow the above, precise plan, this plan is the classical method hammered out over a period of some 2500 years and found to be highly effective. Listeners who familiarize themselves with this format are apt to hear most speeches with increased accuracy.

If we are listening to an informal conversation or discussion, our listening task will be much more difficult if we wish to retain any lasting impressions or find a meaning. Informal discussions may wander around aimlessly with no particular purpose or proposition in mind. A great effort must be made to find the significant ideas and topics mentioned, to remember them through our own restatement of them, and then to try to weave them into a coherent pattern of thought with appropriate conclusions. For example, such a process of listening is especially important in counseling. The counselee's problem may be all but hidden in the rush of his other words, but after listening the astute counselor can frequently pick up recurring themes and repetitions which may ultimately point to the counselee's problem. Thus when one develops proficiency as a listener, he will find it more and more simple to discover the speaker's basic idea or his central proposition, whether in a formal speech or in an informal message.

If we are going to develop an efficient listening method, we must decide to listen sympathetically. Though we may not agree with the speaker, we should demonstrate common courtesy and a genuine interest. The clarity of the speaker's message may depend upon such a response. Negative feedback in the form of an expression of disgust or violent headshaking may so upset a speaker that he may be unable to communicate his true thoughts or feelings. Sympathetic listening will at least help the speaker present his thoughts clearly and forcefully. The listener *then* has the privilege of accepting or rejecting the speaker's ideas.

If we are going to improve our listening method, we must listen critically. Uncritical listeners are easy prey for demagogues. The critical auditor will listen with an open mind, learning to distinguish between important and unimportant ideas. He will train himself to distinguish between fact and inference and not allow emotionally toned words to distract him from central issues. He will be on the lookout for those logical and semantic distortions of language which are barriers to accurate communication.

In recent years the listening factor in communication has been viewed as being at least as important as the sending factor. After all, what is the use of trying to communicate if the receiver is not listening? For the Christian communicator the listening factor becomes tremendously important. Churches are great listening posts. Ministers could significantly increase communication's effectiveness in the church if they were to train their people in the art of good listening. Courses in listening are offered at some colleges and universities. If formal courses are not available, aspiring communicators may profit greatly from the ever-increasing body of literature available in this field.[14]

Summary

Communication is a process. It operates in a circular fashion between speaker and listener. Three types of communication are identifiable — intrapersonal, interpersonal, and group. Intrapersonal communication occurs within an individual. Interpersonal communication occurs between two or more individuals. Group communication involves more than two individuals.

Human communication functions on two levels — nonverbal and verbal. Nonverbal communication may be seen in such things as one's attitudes, actions, and expressions. Verbal communication functions through such communication skills as rhetorical ability, word choice, and vocal ex-

---

[14]See on this subject Ralph G. Nichols and Leonard A. Stevens, *Are You Listening?* (New York: McGraw-Hill Book Company, Inc., 1957); and Ralph G. Nichols and Thomas R. Lewis, *Listening and Speaking A Guide to Effective Oral Communication* (Dubuque, Iowa: Wm. C. Brown Company Publishers, 1954), and others.

pression. Nonverbal and verbal communication may be found in speakers, listeners, and messages.

The four ingredients of any communication process are the speaker, message, channel, and receiver. Put into a functioning unit, they work toward the high fidelity of a message. The communication process always occurs in a space-time relationship. It should continually adjust itself to the total situation.

Chapter Four

Barriers to Communication

PERFECT COMMUNICATION IS A PHANTOM. Messages will never convey exactly the same meaning in the minds of both speakers and listeners. If for no other reason, the individual differences of the participants preclude perfection. The message itself may be true, and still it may not be received by a listener with all of the subtle implications intended by the sender.

Accurate and adequate communication, however, is certainly possible, and this ought to be the constant objective. This attainment of accurate and adequate meaning is difficult because communication must always contend with a host of barriers. Modern discoveries in the physical and social sciences have eliminated many of these blocks, but continued interpersonal tensions indicate that many remain.

Communication barriers are of many kinds. They may be physical, psychological, intellectual, cultural, spiritual, or linguistic. Accordingly, these barriers occur in all three of our "worlds" — the experiential, the evaluational, and the symbolic.

The exceeding complexity of our physical universe with its continual process, endless diversities, numerous similarities, unique relatedness, and unswerving order makes it difficult to comprehend with our finite minds, let alone describe with our limited vocabularies.

The apparent complexity of our spiritual world creates an even more vexing barrier. Men find it easy to agree with empirically demonstrated facts of the physical universe. But they argue endlessly over disagreements about the non-sensory experiences of the spiritual universe. Because of these seemingly insoluble reasons, some advocate the elimination of moral and religious devotion in favor of a strictly scientific approach to life.

The Christian insists that such barriers are not insurmountable. While recognizing the existence of the barriers, the Christian believes that the only way to overcome them is to add to the reality of the physical universe the vital reality of the spiritual universe. Only then does life make sense, and only then will people come to love one another. During the Hitler era Germany was probably as scientifically oriented as any nation in history, but it lacked the spiritual integrity to keep it from plunging the world into a tragic conflict.

The observation and judgment of our experiential world would seem to be such simple functions that they should involve few barriers. On the contrary, these two functions of the evaluative process create many barriers.

Because the observation of life's experiences depends so heavily upon sense perception, it encounters the limitations posed by our senses. Seldom does a life experience engage all of the five senses at once. Individuals experience a great variety of sensitivity of the sense organs, and proximity to an event or object elicits varied responses from different

individuals. The continual process of life's experiences demands adjustment of one's viewpoint. In light of these
factors, human observation is at best partial and limited.
A constant consciousness of such barriers is the first step
toward an enlightened and tolerant philosophy of communication.

Judgment encounters more formidable barriers than observation. General and specific knowledge, individual motivation, values systems, and intensional-extensional orientation all color one's judgment. The relative instability of
these human factors has created communication barriers so
discouraging that many thinkers virtually advocate the ignoring of all matters of value. To these thinkers facts are
stable, and values are relative. Man, according to this
thinking, should be studied as any other material object,
but values should be ignored. Such a view seems to be a
vast oversimplification of man. It ignores man's characteristic purposes, attitudes, and values without which he is no
longer a man. As Harold A. Larrabee so aptly points out,

> To ignore such matters is to produce only a caricature of man
> — a series of propositions about chemical elements and weights
> and reflexes which leaves out everything that is characteristically
> human. The things which are omitted, furthermore, are pre-
> cisely those about which men crave reliable knowledge most
> keenly. They are the *values* which possess all the warmth and
> color and intensity of living. Attested scientific facts are not
> what men "live by" in the intimacies of daily existence.[1]

Yet without depriving man of his unique powers, we can
still work to eliminate objectionable evaluative barriers.
Patient and painstaking observation of life's experiences,
coupled with disciplined yet impartial judgment, will do
much to overcome such barriers.

The impact of man's personal life can be a potential
communication barrier of vast significance. The *ethos*

---

[1]Harold A. Larrabee, *Reliable Knowledge* (Boston: Houghton Mifflin Company, 1945), pp. 600-601.

(character) of a man can be either negative or positive. Negative *ethos* is a barrier to constructive communication. Evil character, bad attitudes, and poor appearance may injure one's effectiveness. Lack of knowledge, poor evaluative powers, and inept communicative skills are equally injurious.

The Christian who wishes to eliminate such barriers should cultivate positive character qualities. High moral standards, healthy attitudes, a favorable appearance, and spiritual maturity greatly contribute to one's communicative power. Wide and detailed knowledge, keen evaluative powers, and skill in conveying messages tend to remove communication barriers.

Although Christians may have become wearied with endless reminders of the truth that positive character qualities will improve their communication, its powerful effect upon the spreading of the Gospel demands its reiteration. Few communication barriers are as impregnable as a poor character. Few spectacles are as incongruous as a timid minister preaching fearlessness or as a lecher expostulating on virtue. People still expect Christians to practice what they preach.

Many misunderstandings between human beings fall into the area of logical and semantic fallacies. These fallacies may be the misstatement of facts, the use of wrong words, or the drawing of wrong inferences. Semanticists are concerned with what men *mean* by what they say. The words, "That was a wonderful sermon, pastor," may be an expression of deep gratitude or a thoughtless verbal cliché. Though there are numerous verbal and nonverbal barriers to communication, one should be acquainted with the most frequently occurring distortions of logic and language.

Allness or Overgeneralization

Allness or overgeneralizing is both an attitude of mind

and a way of speaking. An individual with an allness attitude thinks he knows all there is to know about an object or
event. He frequently closes his mind to new ideas or evidence about a situation saying, "I've already made up my
mind — don't confuse me with the facts." Allness is the
essence of dogmatism, often prematurely precluding discussion on vital issues. Holders of the allness attitude are
brittle and unbending, and thus difficult communication
barriers are created.

The allness attitude leads to fanaticism. Extremists seem
to thrive on inside information which is considered the last
word on ideological, political, and religious issues. These
fanatics imply they are the last line of defense against in-
sidious social and theological infiltration. Dictators, filled
with boundless fanaticism, plunged the world into World
War II, and some of our loved ones lie buried as a result.
The closing phases of World War II in the Pacific drama-
tized such fanatic allness in the *Kamikaze* incidents. Some
of Japan's finest pilots, convinced beyond all doubt that suicide bombing alone could turn the tide of allied victory,
flung themselves and their planes to destruction seeking to
demolish American naval vessels.

The allness attitude is reflected in our language structure.
We use certain words called universals and superlatives.
Such terms as all, always, every, whole, total, none, and no
such are universals of an all-inclusive nature. A slightly
different type of word but one equally loaded with allness
implications is the superlative. Words of extreme degrees of
quality such as best, worst, highest, most, and least give the
impression of having no equal or superior.

Universal and superlative terms are not always wrong
or untrue. The apostle Paul writing to the Romans flatly
stated, "For all have sinned, and come short of the glory of
God" (Romans 3:23). Such an allness is difficult to dis-
prove, and any effort to do so is usually reduced to haggling
over terms. Paul also unequivocally declared to the Co-

rinthians, "But now abideth faith, hope, love, these three; and the greatest of these is love" (I Corinthians 13:13 RSV). Human experience also finds this superlative difficult to surpass. There are other universals and superlatives in human experience which are clearly justifiable. Nevertheless, allness and superlative terms are verbal symbols which when used ought to make one ask, "Is this statement or attitude true?" — "Are there exceptions which should qualify the statement?" — "Is this universally true?"

Pastors and churches grow weary hearing those oft-repeated, allness-oriented clichés such as "All the preacher did was ask for money," or "The church doesn't meet any of my needs." Disruption within the Christian community sometimes centers in such allness attitudes and verbal exchanges. Irreparable damage to interpersonal relationships has followed emotional outbursts such as "I'll never sing another solo as long as that organist is here," or during a church argument when someone claims, "I have all the facts."

There are various forms of allness and over-generalization. We see the closed-mind attitude; the categorizing of individuals, groups, and ideas; the thin-entering-wedge type of generalization where one builds a mountain out of a mole-hill; and the two-valued or either-or orientation. The ability to generalize is a quality of the human mind. It is one of those characteristics distinguishing men from animals. To communicate one must be able to say "bird" and thus refer to a class of living things rather than to have to delineate every species of bird in existence. And yet this very generalizing ability can cause trouble. A type of generalized argument is used by liquor interests when they say that selling whiskey is good for America because it stimulates the nation's economy. Omitted is the fact that liquor causes alcoholism and broken homes, and that local and national agencies have to spend millions of dollars in rehabilitation. This is the weakness of the allness statement.

Care must be taken that general and sometimes drastic conclusions are not drawn from one or two incidents. Energy can be drained by jumping to unwarranted conclusions. These are the kinds of communication barriers that slip between the ranks of Christians and divide them. Only earnest and consistent efforts toward self-discipline can eliminate the blocks to our understanding and put us in effective communication with one another.

The Thin-entering-wedge Statement

A form of allness with which we sometimes come in contact is called the thin-entering-wedge statement. It involves taking one or two incidents and building them into a national catastrophe. J. Edgar Hoover points to this type of reasoning as a favorite communist technique of mass agitation. In describing this tactic he says:

> Thus, seizing upon the inherent desire of all Americans to reduce taxes, the *Daily Worker* editorializes that foreign aid should be curtailed and billions should not be taken "out of our pockets for a new phony 'emergency'."
> . . . The huge seventy-billion a year "defense" budget is rushing America to inflation and economic crisis.[2]

The meaning of the communist paper, that helping a foreign country or bolstering our national defense will lead us to economic crisis and maybe something worse, is obvious and of course false. In the words of Stuart Chase, this is "plotting one or two points, and then riding the curve to cloud cuckooland."[3] This is the process of making a mountain out of a mole hill, or of stirring up a tempest in a tea-cup, and it can have far-reaching results.

This slow building of small incidents or things into a

---

[2]J. Edgar Hoover, *Masters of Deceit* (New York: Holt, Rinehart and Winston, 1958), p. 193.

[3]Stuart Chase in Collaboration with Marion Tyler Chase, *Power of Words* (New York: Harcourt Brace and Company, 1954), p. 12.

large result has occurred enough to make many men extremely edgy. Embezzlers frequently steal money in small but gradually increasing amounts. Wars seldom start at the full-shooting stage. Church splits often start as minor difficulties. To ignore the damaging possibilities of the thin-entering-wedge type of divisiveness is foolish. Nevertheless, the church would be paralyzed if it assumed that every small incident would eventually turn into a major catastrophe.

Some men feel that rigid conformity to doctrinal standards and particular interpretations ought to go beyond the major themes of theology to the minor details of Biblical exegesis. They feel that any deviation from their views at any given point is the tentacle of an octopus which will eventually strangle their whole theological system. Evangelicals, it is true, agree on a general body of theology. They have doctrinal statements which herald to the world what they believe. However, they should not extend those doctrinal statements to the minutest details of Greek verb tenses or word connotations and insist that everyone conform rigidly to such definitions. And this attitude of mind should be carried over to other areas of our theology as well. Where our doctrinal statements allow for differences in interpretation, we should not construe these differences to mean incipient liberalism.

Sometimes the thin-entering-wedge spirit is carried over to denominational cooperation. Combining the thin-entering-wedge attitude with the either-or fallacy, one can consider a person who disagrees with the *status quo* in any policies dangerous and place him into the opposite of two competing camps. This thinking leads to the idea that to allow disagreement is to court disaster. "One rotten apple in the barrel will spoil the whole barrel," cries such thinking. "Down with the opposition!" Yet this very privilege of individual freedom is one of the cardinal tenets of our Christian heritage.

The thin-entering-wedge attitude can enter into our social relationships. At a church conference some time ago the problem of racial integration was being debated. A strong segregationist group within the denomination argued: "The Southern way of life *is* at stake. Those outside the South may, through integration and amalgamation, dilute the pure strain of their progeny into a mulatto strain if they wish to do so."[4] Such a stretching of logic overlooks the social barriers which have kept the vast majority of Negroes and whites apart throughout their entire existence. The integration of Negroes in many sections of our country has not brought about a wholesale breakdown in marriage customs. Extrapolation (the scientific name of this type of prediction) has divided families, friends, groups, and institutions. The divorce courts bulge with couples who have projected two or three incidents into marital incompatability which some judges in turn decide is grounds for divorce.

To avoid the danger of the thin-entering-wedge fallacy, we should constantly ask ourselves whether statements of this type are stretched too far. Though they are not always false, the mature Christian who really desires to evaluate life properly and who wants to communicate must discipline himself to distinguish the true from the exaggerated. Otherwise one might fall into the trap of logic similar to that of the driver who found three gas stations per mile along a stretch of Montreal-bound highway in Vermont and concluded that there would be plenty of gas all the way to the North Pole.

The Either-or Problem

A third type of allness fallacy is often found in the use of the either-or statement. The either-or attitude assumes that everything is either black or white. There is no room

---

[4]News Item in the *Denver Post*, April 28, 1960.

for the middle ground of gray. Aristotle called this the law of the excluded middle. And, as with the other allness factors, there are enough valid cases of the either-or situation to make it a useful tool in communication. Thus Christianity states that a man is either saved or lost, which is correct and scriptural. There is no middle ground of half-saved and half-lost in relation to salvation. And despite the fact that one often jokes about being half-dead at the end of a day's hard work, a man is either dead or alive. Even such a staunch semanticist as Alfred Korzybski allowed for an either-or condition under certain circumstances. He pointed out that under certain conditions where there was no human interference, the survival problem for animals was two-valued and very sharp. The animals, therefore, either survived or died out.[5]

However, the two-valued or either-or condition does not always hold true. In fact, its potential implications and dangers are so subtle and misleading that one must be constantly vigilant lest he misuse it. A man is not invariably either our friend or our enemy. A person is not always either right or wrong. On the contrary, each one of us has found that he can sometimes be both right and wrong, and we resent being forced into the wrong position when we are partly right. While most Christians have held the doctrine of total depravity, they have also been willing to see in the foulest individual a potential for the transforming power of the grace of God. We should not "give up" on any individual regardless of how hopeless he may seem.

Sometimes pastors and churches inadvertently allow their interpersonal relationships to move to such extreme positions that they are confronted with an either-or situation.

---

[5]Alfred Korzybski, *Science and Sanity: An Introduction to Non-Aristotelian Systems and General Semantics* (third edition; Lakeville, Connecticut: The International Non-Aristotelian Library Publishing Company, 1948), pp. 335-336.

One minister said concerning the chairman of his board during several successive pastorates, "There isn't room enough in this church for both of us. Either he or I must go!" In every case the pastor ended up leaving the church.

Debate can turn out to be sharply two-valued and is frequently divisive. Let a question come before a business meeting, and reason is sometimes lost. Supporters line up on the supposed two sides of the issue crying, "After all, there are always two sides to a question, aren't there?" And this despite the fact that the question may have more than two sides so that settling it with a simple yes or no may distort its true nature.

More serious than distorting the question, however, is the possible tension created between the debating parties. Men may become bitter enemies, castigating one another and assassinating one another's characters.

All of this communication breakdown occurs because a many-sided question has been hammered down into a two-sided one. For example, in America's predominantly two-party political system, Presidential election campaigns seldom start with an either-or choice between just two candidates. During the Presidential primaries our two major parties may have a dozen or more Presidential hopefuls competing for nomination and the eventual election. At the primary stage of the campaign, Americans are confronted with a multi-valued choice of candidates. Then after the major political parties have held their nominating conventions, Americans are confronted with a realistic either-or choice for the final election. In such a political system it is foolish to argue heatedly over whether one or another Presidential hopeful will win the election before the major parties have held their nominating conventions. After the two major parties have named their official candidates, there is plenty of time to argue whether a Republican or Democrat will be the next President of the United States.

We cannot eliminate debating either from society in general or from church meetings in particular simply because a debate may assume a sharp yes or no decision. But we can look carefully at each question being debated, each argument used, each decision being sought to determine whether or not a simple vote of for or against oversimplifies the total situation and makes a two-valued problem out of a many-valued one. Furthermore, we can discipline ourselves to realize that when a man argues on the opposite side of a question from that for which we stand, he is not automatically our enemy, hating us or even disliking us. Such a conclusion would have to be based on much more evidence than a simple disagreement.

A recognition of life's multi-valued character will help in surmounting the either-or communication barrier. When confronted with a many-valued situation, one must evaluate it as such. When faced with a true either-or choice, one must recognize it and choose accordingly. Communication is distorted when a many-valued situation is shrunk into a two-valued choice.

Invalid Cause and Effect

One of the most natural and logical processes of the human mind is that of relating causes to happenings. It is said that prohibition causes bootlegging. Others claim that progressive education is behind the growing juvenile delinquency problem. Or in the area of theology we hear charges that Calvinism leads to dead orthodoxy, or that Arminianism leads to social emphasis and social emphasis in turn leads to liberalism. Thus causes are continually being related to effects as attempts are made to explain events.

Cause and effect reasoning has a good and respectable history and is a process used by the curious mind. It has led many to a deep conviction concerning the existence of God. Common sense is found in the argument that just as a fine watch must have been manufactured by an expert watchmaker, so our complex universe must have been created by an intelligent being far superior to any human being. Proper education of our boys and girls in Christian truth usually causes strong, clean character. As a result the Sunday school and other Christian education facilities exist. The implications of cause and effect reasoning are broad, deep, and penetrating.

Nevertheless, this very cause and effect reasoning process can be fallaciously used. In searching for reasons behind events we can and do often settle on the wrong causes or only part of the right causes. Just because one event occurs before another, this does not necessarily mean that the first event caused the second. For example, when an impatient driver races his motor before the traffic light turns green, the first action did not cause the second. This type of error is described as the *post hoc ergo propter hoc* error meaning "after it, therefore because of it." More often it is referred to as *post hoc* reasoning.

When *post hoc* reasoning is demonstrated, its weakness is obvious. However, the error is not always easily seen. For many years medical researchers suspected that excessive tobacco smoking was causing a rise in lung cancer among smokers. Tests were conducted and articles on smoking and health were reported in leading magazines. So concerned were the tobacco interests that they contributed sums of money for research projects of their own which they hoped to use to offset the medical reports. And they were partially successful in trying to brand the medical findings as *post hoc* reasoning. Tobacco researchers tried to show that lung cancer could be produced by factors other than their product. Thus polluted air, smog, factory smoke, and various other foreign matters were involved, they claimed. Yet medical science relentlessly pursued its experiments. Evidence linking smoking to lung cancer piled up in almost irrefutable volume. Now it is quite generally conceded that a cause and effect relationship exists between the two and that no *post hoc* fallacy is involved. Tobacco producers scramble to produce filters, providing mute evidence of the effectiveness of medical research's willingness to track down a cause regardless of what it involves.

Such careful persistence is needed in Christian circles. For Christians are not immune to the fallacy of *post hoc* logic. The necessity of determining causes behind events must be constantly faced. Why is church attendance on Sunday evenings declining? What is causing renewed religious interest across the country while crime, immorality, and international tensions are mounting? The causes of church splits should be known precisely, and flimsy evidence which might be offered as the cause for pastoral failures or short-term ministries must not be tolerated. If there are tensions and misunderstandings within churches, a few hasty explanations are not enough. All of these problems are susceptible to the fallacy of *post hoc* reasoning. Incorrect or inadequate causes assigned to the problems can create irreparable damage to individuals and groups.

Lying with Statistics

The tendency of American people to worship numbers is almost unbelievable. A Frenchman once remarked that Americans like ice cream and statistics, as both slip down so easily.[6] Christians in this American population are no exception to this. Given an impressive table, chart, or graph of precise figures, we believe a fact is supported

---

[6]As reported by Stuart Chase, *Guides to Straight Thinking with 13 Common Fallacies* (New York: Harper & Brothers Publishers, 1956), p. 97.

because it appears on the surface to be an indisputable fact. The problem lurking here is that figures don't always prove a fact. Statistics can and do often become misleading either innocently or deliberately. So susceptible are statistics to this weakness that there is a recent book with the arresting title, *How to Lie with Statistics.*[7] This book shows how the use of the statistical method of treating data can be prostituted to lead to misleading and dishonest communication.

The varieties of statistical abuse are numerous and in some instances quite technical. Therefore we will discuss only those that are encountered most frequently in our Christian circles, tending to disrupt our communication processes.

What is average? Frequently we hear the term average attached to various and sundry observations made by experts or non-experts. We hear someone say, "The average Christian wants to be told what to believe, not stimulated to think for himself." Closely aligned to this observation is another common one encountered by many pastors, "The average church member wants a sermon pitched on the level of a twelve-year-old so everybody can understand it." Pet peeves, subtle criticisms, and outright distortions are often justified by the use of the adjective average. The average church is irrelevant, the average church member is a hypocrite, or the average preacher is a money grabber: these are fairly common distortions.

A true average can be discovered for almost any set of opinions. Sometimes this average is easily obtained, but at other times it is extremely difficult to determine. The trouble with averages such as those mentioned above is they contain what is called "the sample with the built-in-bias."[8]

---

[7]Darrell Huff, *How to Lie with Statistics* (New York: W. W. Norton & Co., 1954).

[8]*Ibid.*, p. 11.

For example, take the statement, "The average Christian wants to be told what to believe." Valid questions immediately arise. Which Christians stated that they wanted to be told what to believe? Are those who made such statements representative of all Christians or are they merely one element? And if they are just one element, then how large an element are they? Is the one reporting this observation guilty of talking only with those who agree with this view, or has he taken a true random sample of opinions? The same biased view can appear in observations about low-level sermons or the irrelevance of the church. Two problems arise here. One has to do with how representative the sampling of opinion actually is, and the other has to do with the percentage of the total number of constituents who were sampled. If only those were questioned who held one view, then the average would be biased. If only a small percent of the total number of church members or pastors were polled concerning an issue, then an average could hardly be established. Be careful about characterizing the average man.

Distorted Graphs. Most churches at one time or another have used charts or graphs to portray some kind of financial or institutional progress. Their value in showing progress is obvious. It would seem impossible to distort the communicative power of a cold statistical graph. But it is possible to distort a graph so that the unwary mind of an individual, untutored in the ways of statistics, will not catch its error.

Even though the same figures may be used, manipulation of the scales on a graph can create differences in its appearance. For example, suppose two Sunday school officers were debating attendance progress over a five-year period. One officer, desiring to make the advance look spectacular, plots a graph with a narrow time scale and a long numerical scale. The result would look like the top graph on the opposite page.

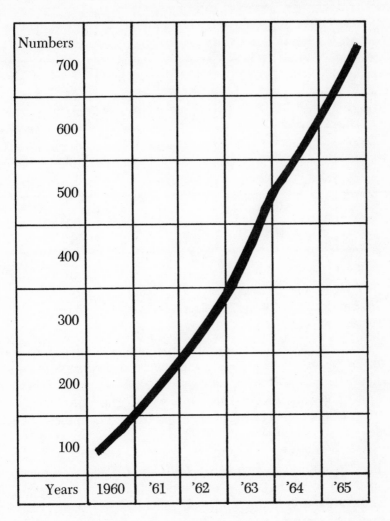

Numbers						
700						
600						
500						
400						
300						
200						
100						
Years	1960	'61	'62	'63	'64	'65

His opponent wishes to play down the progress. Even though he may use exactly the same attendance figures, he can make the progress ascent look much less spectacular. By plotting a graph with a broader time axis and a shorter numerical axis, he can create the second graph on the following page.

Numbers						
1000						
800						
600						
400						
200						
0						
Years	1960	'61	'62	'63	'64	'65

Statistics can be misleading if one is not aware they can be misused. Many an enterprising promoter has sold his product by the use of such distorted graphs.[9]

The Annual Report. Another potential statistical trap we often fall into in churches is the one connected with the annual report. Most churches produce one of these reports, and rightly so. As good stewards of the grace of God, they need to give an account of their ministry. But these reports sometimes become tools of innocent or contrived deceit. Numerical totals, including conversions, baptisms, and membership additions, frequently tell one rosy story in an annual report while the facts they describe portray something drastically different. A church may look on paper like a tower of strength to a prospective pastor. However, a few months as pastor of that church may produce a sadly different picture. Similarly the report of service sent by a pastoral candidate to a church considering him may look statistically either promising or disappointing when in re-

[9]*Ibid.,* p. 60.

ality the man may be greatly different than the statistics of his report reveal.

Some contemporary evangelists appear to be snared in this unfortunate trap. The current preoccupation with the philosophy of results has made popular the evangelist who persuades the most people to tread the sawdust trail. Some evangelists have succumbed to this church and pastoral preoccupation with statistics and have either padded their reports or, worse yet, have adopted questionable rhetorical and psychological gimmicks to get people forward in meetings. This vicious circle, if continued, can only ruin our communication privilege, for it makes the church look cheap in the eyes of the world. Christians ought always to avoid even the appearance of evil. Church membership rolls must be continually revised to reveal the true situation as clearly as possible. Annual statistical reports ought to be as nearly correct maps of the territory they represent as they can be made. And the study of statistical reports should be pursued with the realization that they do not tell all the story.

The study of statistics can be most important if such factors as population trends or property cost rises are being studied preliminary to the building of a new church. An area which may have been growing rapidly for months or even years may suddenly slow down. One cannot always take the figures and through the procedure of extrapolation (projecting these figures into the future) come out with a correct prognostication. Such figuring must always be qualified by saying that, all other things being equal, the trend may go on.

Suppose a church has grown from one or two hundred to a thousand members in ten years under the same pastor who then resigned and went elsewhere. For this church to assume that its previous yearly increase would automatically continue so that in another ten or twelve years its membership would reach two thousand might be foolish. Furthermore, for it to expect the next pastor to accomplish such a feat might be not only risky but unrealistic and unfair. While the practice of extrapolation is easily worked out on paper or with a slide rule, when applied to real life, it becomes unusually tricky.

Mark Twain once lampooned the questionable practice of extrapolation in his book, *Life on the Mississippi*:

> In the space of one hundred and seventy-six years the Lower Mississippi has shortened itself two hundred and forty-two miles. That is, an average of a trifle over one mile and a third per year. Therefore, any calm person, who is not blind or idiotic, can see that in the Old Oolitic Silurian Period, just a million years ago next November, the lower Mississippi River was upwards of one million three hundred thousand miles long, and stuck out over the Gulf of Mexico like a fishing-rod. And by the same token any person can see that seven hundred and forty-two years from now the Lower Mississippi will be only a mile and three quarters long, and Cairo and New Orleans will have joined their streets together, and be plodding comfortably along under a single mayor and a mutual board of aldermen. There is something fascinating about science. One gets such wholesale returns of conjecture out of such a trifling investment of fact.[10]

Distorted Definitions

Many of us have known those who in the midst of an argument demand their opponents to "define terms." In theological discussions frequently heard is the statement, "If people would only define their terms, there wouldn't be so much misunderstanding." At first this appears to be based on obvious and logical observations. Unfortunately the practice of accurate definition isn't as simple as it may seem. For while it ought certainly to be adopted, the method can become difficult and sometimes deceitful. There are several ways in which error can occur in the use of definitions.

---

[10]Mark Twain, *Life on the Mississippi* (New York: The Heritage Press, 1944), pp. 114-15.

In the first place, one can err by avoiding the practice altogether. For though defining what is meant may have its pitfalls, to omit or evade the obligation is worse yet. The discussion of such words as faith, trust, separation, liberalism, fundamentalism, morality, liberty, bigotry, and many others without letting people know how those terms are being used at the precise time and in the specific context in which they are being used is to confuse, mislead, and even frustrate adequate communication. At least some sincere effort should be made to explain as clearly and as honestly as possible what is meant by the words.

There is another way in which an error can be made in the use of definitions. This is defining in vague and abstract words. Sometimes this happens when one tries to explain certain words by using other words. It can be confusing to look up the meaning of a word such as apathy and find it defined indifference, and then when looking up the meaning of indifference, we find it defined as apathy.

Usually the practice of defining terms vaguely is done innocently and unconsciously. At other times the vagueness of definition is deliberate. For example, many of the divorce suits in our courts today list the almost meaningless term incompatibility as the supposed cause, and the phrase mental cruelty is almost as popular. These have become verbal catch-alls with which almost any dissatisfied spouse in some states can divest himself or herself of an unwanted companion. The vague definition of terms has been at the root of much of the theological controversy between liberals and conservatives during both the past and present. A deliberate vagueness when defining words and phrases for ulterior purposes is wrong whether done by Christian or non-Christian.

A third misuse of definition encountered now and then is sometimes called arbitrary definition. Here a speaker or writer, eager to persuade his audience, defines his terms and phrases the way he wishes them defined. He is like

Humpty-Dumpty whose conversation with Alice in Wonderland went something like this:

> Humpty-Dumpty said: "There's Glory for you." "I don't know what you mean by Glory," Alice said. Humpty-Dumpty smiled contemptuously. "Of course you don't — till I tell you. I meant, there's a nice knock-down argument for you." "But 'glory' doesn't mean 'a nice knock-down argument,'" Alice objected. "When I use a word," Humpty-Dumpty said in a rather scornful tone, "It means just what I choose it to mean, neither more nor less."[11]

The danger of the practice of arbitrary definition in both theological disputes and interpersonal communication is obvious. There are many Biblical and theological words and phrases that are highly abstract and therefore subject to differences in interpretation. To give these words one meaning only is to violate their very nature and to confuse communication. Sometimes even a dictionary can be misleading. These authoritative references arrive at their definitions of words by determination of how words are used. Varying uses for a given word have been found, and the dictionary is bound to list the variable meanings. However, no dictionary can arbitrarily define a word with one meaning when the context of that word suggests another meaning. One would therefore experience only confusion in looking up the word drive unless he knew whether he was using it in the sense of driving a car, driving a golf ball, or raising money in a financial drive.

The abstract nature and the different uses of many words can put the tool of arbitrary definition into the hands of unscrupulous men. The practice of arbitrary definition is often linked with emotional language and labeling designed to blacken the character of individuals. It makes a

---

[11]Lewis Carroll, *Through the Looking-Glass,* p. 123-4 in *Alice's Adventures in Wonderland and Through the Looking Glass* (New York: The Macmillan Company, 1929).

difference whether you call a pastor a shepherd of his flock,
or a domineering dictator. We don't mind our children
being called youngsters, but we bristle if they are labeled
brats.

Sometimes people will go to great lengths to define arbitrarily and label others. One woman was heard by the
author to describe a church as liberal because the members
of that church danced, smoked, and played cards. Such
activities are sometimes found in liberal churches; however,
this is not the generally accepted meaning of liberalism in
churches. Theological liberalism is normally associated with
unbelief concerning such Biblical doctrines as the full inspiration and entire trustworthiness of the Scriptures, the deity
of Christ, the Virgin Birth, His vicarious atonement and
bodily resurrection. Labeling a church as liberal because
some of its members may engage in dancing or smoking
could do harm to the work of Christ.

There is too much of this type of arbitrary definition
and emotional labeling in Christian circles today. The
terms liberal, neo-orthodox, neo-evangelical, pre-millenar-
ian, and many others are being arbitrarily defined and
fastened on individuals and organizations in irresponsible
and sometimes harmful ways. As a result the seeds of
suspicion, enmity, and hatred are sown within Christian
ranks, and communication becomes impossible.

As Christians let us not be guilty of arbitrary definitions, either in personal relationships or in using the Word
of God. Let us be like Paul who could honestly say to the
Corinthians that he was ". . . not walking in craftiness,
nor handling the Word of God deceitfully . . ." (II Corinthians 4:2). Unfortunately there are too many in Christian circles who insist that the Word of God means nothing
until they get through making it mean what they want it to
mean. Difference of opinion and variety in interpretation
are brushed aside, and communication breaks down. All
Christians should be honor-bound to determine what a word

or phrase or situation means within its total context by using the soundest hermeneutic and semantic principles.

False Analogy

At least as early as the fourth century B.C. Aristotle in his *Rhetoric* designated the analogy as one of the topics of enthymemes which, in turn, were a form of reasoning.[12] John Stuart Mill defined the analogy by saying, "Two things resemble each other in one or more respects; a certain proposition is true of one; therefore it is true of the other."[13]

Analogies fall into two general categories, literal and figurative. A comparison between two students, two seminaries, or two churches would be a literal comparison. When the comparison between two objects is so remotely related that it falls into different order systems, it is figurative. To say that preaching the Gospel is like sowing seed in a garden is to compare figuratively one activity with another.

The use of analogy in the pursuit of argument has a long and successful history. William James was right when he said, "Men, taken historically, reason by analogy long before they have learned to reason by abstract characters."[14] And Harold Larrabee pays tribute to its effectiveness when he says: "What we do when we use analogy in making an hypothesis is to utilize the success of a previous ordering of Nature in making a new one."[15]

Analogy makes clear to the listener the abstract idea of the speaker. The beauty of a good and sound analogy is well established. Christ used it frequently for the purpose of teaching abstract, unfamiliar truths in the concrete terms

---

[12]Lane Cooper, trans., *The Rhetoric of Aristotle* (New York: D. Appleton Century and Company, 1932), p. 167.

[13]John Stuart Mill, *System of Logic* (8th ed.) Book III, Chap. XX, par. 2 (New York: Longmans, Green and Co., Inc., 1872).

[14]William James, *The Principles of Psychology* (New York: Henry Holt and Company, 1890), II, p. 363.

[15]Harold Larrabee, *op. cit.*, p. 183.

of the familiar. Who can forget the Matthew parables of the sower who went forth to sow, or of the enemy who sowed tares among the wheat? Who can ever erase from our minds His vivid metaphors — "Ye art the salt of the earth . . ." (Matthew 5:13); "Ye are the light of the world . . ." (Matthew 5:14); or that more extended simile in Matthew 7:24-27 in which He likens men to those who build their houses on rocks or sand depending upon their wisdom in listening to Him?

Men have been quick to seize upon analogy as an instrument of rhetoric. Thus it is necessary to call attention to the vulnerability of the analogy. Despite many advantages, it is not without its possible weaknesses.

False analogies crop up around us everywhere. They find fertile soil in the Christian church as well as out of it. Every now and then one may hear the old saying, "Where there's smoke, there's fire." If this seemingly logical and vivid analogy is misapplied, it can cause irreparable damage. Used in connection with a rumor, it often causes the rumor to stick viciously; and the absence of proof for the rumor will not always clear the accused. Like painting the face with iodine, the application is easy — the removal is extremely difficult. On the surface, the logic of the smoke analogy is irresistible. Where true smoke rises, fire must always exist. The figure is sound. The use of this analogy however with a person rumored to be guilty of some act or thought may be entirely wrong. Let us suppose, for example, that you, the reader of this book, are the pastor of a local church. And let us suppose that someone who bitterly dislikes you starts passing an unfounded rumor around your congregation that you are misappropriating money from the Sunday offerings. How would you like to have the chairman of your Deacon Board ask you to explain the current rumor of misappropriated funds on the basis of that good old philosophical analogy, "Pastor, we believe you are a fine man, but you know as well as we do that where there's smoke there just has to be some fire"? This type of false analogical reasoning stems from thinking that "People just wouldn't be saying things like this if there weren't some truth in it." This approach follows the infamous philosophy of Adolf Hitler that if a lie is big enough and told repeatedly enough people are sure to believe it sooner or later. This is the tragedy of the false analogy. And as a result of this type of thinking one's character as well as his job might be ruined. The above illustration is hypothetical. But the chances of its happening are not only possible, but in many sad instances have been real.

Some time ago a false analogy reared its head in a local church business meeting. The church was without a pastor and was anxiously seeking one. The congregation was divided over the issue of whether to call a man quickly and get the search over with, or to take its time and check the pastoral field thoroughly before voting. During the argument one man jumped to his feet to plead for calling a pastor quickly. "Don't you know," he said, "that a body without a head will die?" This graphic analogy electrified the audience, and its peculiar logic won the day. The church decided to call a man quickly. No one will deny that beheading an individual is always a one-hundred-percent effective way of killing him. But beyond that indisputable fact the only similarity between a headless physical body and a church without a pastor is in the words that are used to describe both. A physical body without a head will, of course, die immediately. A church without a pastor may suffer but can go on living and serving its community indefinitely. This is an illustration of the weakness of the argument by analogy.

An analogy may clarify an argument or occasionally may be used to prove one. And while the clarifying power of an analogy may be valid, the proving ability never is. A point can never be proven by analogy. The analogy then is of great value in communication, but it is also vulnerable to misuse. False analogy occurs when too few similarities are present, when comparison is based on insignificant details, when important differences are disregarded, when no causal relationship can be seen, or when avowed facts are inaccurate.

Proper argument from analogy occurs when a factual basis for comparison is laid; proper causal relationships between objects or events are established; differences as well as similarities are recognized; comparisons are built on strong points of similarities; and comparisons are representative and not isolated.

Analogies are *bona fide* instruments of communication meriting much use. We need to work hard to make sure the analogies we use are not distorted.

Appeal to Authority

There are at least three basic reasons why people believe anything. The first of these depends on direct experience. Often heard are, "Seeing is believing," or "The proof of the pudding is in the eating." The logic of belief based on direct experience appears to be unassailable. Allowing for certain isolated exceptions to such a rule, it is true that direct experience is a basic reason for belief. There can be little doubt, for example, that taking people to see slum conditions is more persuasive than trying to convince them verbally of the existence of such conditions.

The second reason for believing anything has to do with reasoning. Thus having confronted a group of individuals with facts concerning the condition of slum areas, a speaker may use verbal argument to convince the group that they have a responsibility to vote for slum clearance. Here again reason if used sanely is a sound and acceptable reason for belief.

The third reason for believing anything has to do with authority. "I was told it was true," or "The doctor told me

I had measles; therefore, it must be true." Or, again, "The best authorities agree on this interpretation so it must be sound." Many an auditor or reader, unsold by either solid logic or glittering rhetoric, has been firmly convinced by a well-chosen quotation from a famous writer or a well-known authority. On the whole the appeal to authority, like the appeals to direct experience and logical reasoning, is an acceptable reason for belief. However, potential fallacies exist in all three, and such potential fallacies are very common in the appeal to authority. Authorities can be wrong. Most of us speak or write continuously about matters concerning which we lack first-hand evidence. We have not actually had direct experience with the situation or notion we are describing. Moreover, first-hand information or experience may be difficult or actually impossible to obtain. As a result, we necessarily rely upon the observations and opinions of others. We relied upon the reports of newsmen concerning the assassination of John F. Kennedy. Sermons are illustrated with incidents from church history as recorded by an authority such as Kenneth Scott Latourette in his *A History of Christianity*. Consequently library shelves are lined with the best theological, historical, and other authoritative works possible. We use the statements of authorities convincingly in communication, for they have a power all their own. Most of us are aware that many people believe anything in print.

There are various types of authority. There is, for example, the prestige authority, an authority well-known to the audience. In this case, the authority's fame is transferred to his judgment. He may be an expert authority in his field such as Winston Churchill in the field of history. He may not be an authority in other fields. Thus while we would read respectfully Churchill's books on history, we would question him as an authority on the verbal inspiration of the Bible. Nevertheless, his testimony concerning his practice of prayer hits us with a convincing impact.

There is also lay authority. Lay authority is the opinion of the vast numbers of people who are not famous, but who because they make up our great consumer population are considered valuable authorities on needs and wants. As a result, public opinion polls often give national publicity to statements of ordinary individuals. This type of opinion may be representative of either individual or grouped lay authority. A prominent lay citizen may claim the church he attends is the best; a politician returning from a cross-country speaking tour may testify as to grouped lay opinion on certain issues.

Such is the general nature and use of authority. As direct experience and logical reasoning do, the use of authority has a venerable and valuable history. But authorities can be wrong. Most of us would not think to question the learned Pliny. Yet this wise man of old once announced apparently in all seriousness, "I find that a cold is checked by anyone who will kiss the nostrils of a mule."[16] We would quickly agree — concerning this cold remedy — authorities can be wrong. Or, consider the venerable scholar, the renowned Francis Bacon, who once argued persuasively that because of the similarity of the material, a wooden arrow would penetrate the side of a ship to a greater depth than one tipped with iron.[17] Here again in this age of scientific experimentation and refined logic we would be forced to admit — authorities can be wrong.

What are conclusions that can be reached? For one thing the piling up of authoritative quotes to support a favorite argument or cherished doctrine may succeed in doing little more than creating enough distractive noise to drown out the voice of truth. Many a book, article, term paper, or speech takes on the air of impenetrable truth

---

[16]As reported by Irving J. Lee in *Language Habits in Human Affairs* (New York: Harper & Brothers, 1941), p. 117.

[17]*Ibid.*, pp. 117-18.

simply because the communicator has buried his audience in reams of carefully documented and footnoted quotations. The practice of citing every scholar from Confucius to Kierkegaard may be impressive, but it is not necessarily indisputable.

Quotations from authorities can and often do cancel each other. Thus while a whole echelon of Biblical scholars can be cited to prove one view of Christology, another equally impressive group can be assembled to prove the opposite. The answer to the problem in this case is to be found in the Biblical proof itself, not in the positions of authorities.

Sometimes one authority has expressed himself so voluminously that he provides material seemingly contradictory within itself. How else could both Calvinistic and Arminian theologians find such strong support from the same books in the New Testament?

Appeal to authority is necessary and helpful in spite of its potential weaknesses. The use of such appeal must be accompanied with a great effort to use it properly. Various criteria for valid authoritative argument have been constructed. The following list drawn up by A. Craig Baird is representative and helpful.

(1) Is the authority competent? (2) Is the authority prejudiced? (3) Is the authority reliable? (4) Is the authority definite? (5) Is the authority supported by other sources? (6) Is the authority supported by argument from specific instances, causal relation, and analogy?[18]

Such rigid checking will not always be possible. However, whenever possible a check on the validity of the authority being used should be made. Otherwise clarion

---

[18]From *Argumentation, Discussion, and Debate* by A. Craig Baird (Copyright 1959 by McGraw-Hill Book Co., Inc., 1959), p. 149. Used by permission.

notes of truth can be distorted by the high-sounding tones of mere authoritative noise.

Begging the Question

The communication of truth may be distorted by other faulty reasoning processes. Reasoning is a valid type of proof as long as it is sound; yet reasoning is not infallible. There are enough ways of mutilating the reasoning process sufficiently so people are misled. Prominent among these ways are the series of distortions called begging the question. "To beg the question," according to Ketcham, "is to assume its truth or falsity without proof."[19] Or, in the words of R. W. Sellars, "In an argument, it consists in taking for granted what an opponent would not admit if its significance were understood; it is the covert assumption of a truth you are pretending to prove."[20]

The process of begging the question is accomplished in at least three ways. Oftentimes it takes the form of arguing in circles. Thus, a student is urged to study the courses in philosophy at Harvard University because they are the best in the country. When the student asks why they are the best in the country, he is told they are the best because they are given at Harvard University. A close look at this apparent reasoning process will reveal that no actual evidence is given for the high quality of the philosophy courses. Instead, the conclusion is made that Harvard is best because it is best. Such a verbal merry-go-round gives one the distinct impression of being caught in a revolving door. This communication evasion, argument in a circle, can distract our attention from truth in far more serious

---

[19]Victor Alvin Ketcham, *The Theory and Practice of Argumentation and Debate* (New York: The Macmillan Company, 1914), p. 149.

[20]R. W. Sellars, *The Essentials of Logic* (Boston: Houghton Mifflin Company, 1945), p. 154.

ways. Felix Adler once exposed this fallacy in a spirited argument against child labor:

> There is an argument in favor of child-labor so un-American and so inhuman that I am almost ashamed to quote it, and yet it has been used, and I fear it is secretly in the minds of some who would not openly stand for it. A manufacturer standing near the furnace of a glasshouse and pointing to a procession of young Slav boys who were carrying the glass on trays, remarked, "Look at their faces, and you will see that it is idle to take them from the glasshouse in order to give them an education; they are what they are, and will always remain what they are." He meant that there are some human beings — and these Slavs of the number — who are mentally irredeemable, so fast asleep intellectually that they cannot be awakened; designed by nature, therefore, to be hewers of wood and drawers of water. This cruel and wicked thing was said of Slavs; it is the same thing which has been said from time immemorial by the slave-owners of their slaves. First they degrade human beings by denying them the opportunity to develop their better nature: no schools, no teaching, no freedom, no outlook; and then, as if in mockery, they point to the degraded condition of their victims as a reason why they should never be allowed to escape from it.[21]

Though this illustration may seem far removed from us personally because child labor is now a dead issue in our culture, the fallacious reasoning process itself is not dead. On several recent occasions this arguing in a circle has been applied to the segregation problem between whites and Negroes. The verbal battles center around the crucial points of the Negro's supposed educational and religious inferiority. No one using the argument in a circle would allow for the possibility that the Negroes might be scholastically inferior because they have been continually denied the type of education that would make them equal with the whites. No one was stating that the Negro's religious practices might be different from ours simply because he has

---

[21]Felix Adler, *The Annals of the American Academy of Political and Social Science.* May, 1905; Vol. XXV, No. 3.

been denied the right to learn the ways of the white Christian. This type of circular reasoning contributes to the Negro's alleged inferiority by denying him that which would make him equal. Then, adding insult to injury, this inferiority is used as the reason the Negro cannot be allowed to better himself. A pastor once withdrew his church's financial support from a Christian school, thus handicapping the school in its forward progress. Then he openly avowed that his refusal to support the school was because it was not making progress. Such reasoning helped him slide out the same door which he had opened to let himself in, argumentatively speaking. Argument in a circle is a particularly vicious practice anywhere and especially so in Christian circles.

The practice of assuming the truth of a proposition is closely associated with argument in circles; both are ways of begging the question. Sometimes the assumption of the truth of a proposition takes the form of seemingly self-evident truths. Self-evident truths are statements the truth of which are suggested or assumed but not proved. Such self-evident truths are often prefaced with such statements as "Everybody knows . . ." or "It goes without saying . . ." Actually, everyone may not know what the speaker is about to claim; whatever truth he may be about to advance may not "go without saying." Such truths need to be proved not assumed.

Frequently the castor oil of self-evident truth is disguised in the orange juice of age-old proverbs and poured down the throat of an unsuspecting audience. Thus such statements as "Everybody knows that haste makes waste" receive general acceptance. Unfortunately, such homespun philosophy is cancelled by the equally accepted, "Any school boy knows that he who hesitates is lost."

Self-evident truths can be communicated within the slogans themselves. Many a church has atrophied waiting for history to repeat itself. And too often a great missionary cause has floundered upon the rock of miserliness which in turn is based on the philosophy that "Fools rush in where angels fear to tread." What preacher has not felt the whiplash of some careless member saying, "Why is it that preacher's kids are always the worst?" Such use of self-evident truths needs to be proved, not swallowed without examination.

Another statement which smacks of the self-evident truth error is, "Once a criminal always a criminal"; this one can defeat an ex-convict out again in society before he has a chance to get a fresh start. Despite psychologists who have been telling us for years that we need not stop learning, that our capacity to acquire new knowledge drops no more than one percent a year one hears quite commonly, "You can't teach an old dog new tricks."

A communicator can beg the question through the insertion of certain emotionally packed words in an otherwise legitimate sentence. Notice how the following statements prejudice the reader or hearer because of the implications of the italicized words:

> We must fight the *greedy* plans of the employers.
> We should not vote for this *compromise* motion.
> Should students *waste* their time studying languages?
> The *repulsive* doctrine of total depravity is no longer acceptable.
> The *true-blue* character of his life demands that you listen to him.

Begging the question happens more often than we may realize. Its effect is powerful, and its method subtle because it is accomplished by the potent vehicle of suggestion. Suggestion bypasses both critical evaluation and logical analysis and convinces the will without resorting to use of the intellect. Suggestion can be in responsible hands a valid conveyor of truth. But it can also bolster invalid reasoning. Unfortunately, suggestion, like any other vehicle, can carry harmful as well as helpful cargo.

History's most notorious question-begging incident took place early one First-Century morning in the judgment hall of Pontius Pilate. Certain infuriated Jews had led Christ there to secure His death sentence from the ex-slave now enthroned as Roman ruler. But Pilate, carefully protecting himself, probed for their motives with the pointed question, "What accusation bring ye against this man?" (John 18: 29). And their reply bluntly side-stepped this issue. "If he were not a malefactor, we would not have delivered him up unto thee" (John 18:30). The charge brought against Christ needed to be proved, not merely assumed. Yet with such twisted logic, His accusers saw to it that the Son of God was crucified.

Name Calling

Men have discovered that they can harm others by attaching labels to them. Name calling, or invective as this practice is sometimes called, consists of using derogatory value labels with an individual or idea. The purpose is to influence others' judgment by attributing a characteristic which listeners will despise to an individual or idea. The terms isolationist, radical, fellow traveler, bigot, and others have been and are being used to disparage politicians and international figures. In religious circles such terms as compromiser, modernist, and fundamentalist are sometimes used to deride individuals. Such invective is harmful to the Christian witness.

The practice of encomium or panegyric is the opposite extreme to namecalling or invective. Encomium is the expression of lavish praise and consists mainly of the application of explicit labels denoting approval or the presence of highly laudable qualities. Organizations or individuals who are given to this excessive form of "whitewashing" of their own groups or of other individuals may curtail their effectiveness by practicing such logical error.

The effectiveness of labeling or name calling can be questioned. With certain people it will carry weight. With others its success will depend upon the extent to which evidence is submitted justifying the accusations. After all, there is no harm done in calling a murderer by that name if he is guilty. The vicious practice we should avoid, however, is that which unjustly labels a man, an idea, or an organization in such a way as deliberately to create a wrong impression in the minds of an unsuspecting audience. The effectiveness of slanted terms whose capacity to evoke value judgments from an audience has been coldly calculated cannot be denied. As A. P. Herbert once put it, "Give your political dog a cleverly bad name, and it may do him more harm than many sound arguments."[22] The practice of name calling has no place in accepted communication procedure.

Attacking the Man

One of the most unjust of logical fallacies is that of attacking a man instead of his ideas. Because their cases have been weak, unethical lawyers have been known to criticize their legal opponents instead of the points of the case being tried. Politicians sometimes attack an opponent's character instead of his platform or policies. Such tactics are not confined to the legal or political world. They may be observed in all phases of life.

The argument against the man is often hooked up with the fallacies of name calling and guilt by association. During the 1960 Presidential election *ad hominem* arguments filled the air. The much-feared possibility of a Catholic in the White House was not only a case of guilt by association but became in some cases little more than *ad hominem* attack. Because of the nature of John F. Kennedy's religion it became exceedingly difficult to separate a logical analysis

---

[22]A. P. Herbert, *What a Word* (New York: Doubleday and Company, Inc., 1936), p. 229.

of his position from personal abuse. However his avowed rejection of relation between Church and State convinced many and they voted for him with confidence: The American people had every right to attack and reject a Roman Catholic President who would identify the Church with the State. But when the candidate openly and repeatedly denied personal belief in such a doctrine, then further attack upon him at that point became *ad hominem.* Had President Kennedy allowed himself to get involved in activities or legislation in which he contradicted his stated position, however, then attack could have logically resumed, on the issue not the man.

In Christian circles today personal attack is widespread and harmful. It painfully manifests itself in the anti-intellectualism which has settled down over some groups like a fog. Under the blanket of fog the in-fighting frequently moves away from facts and centers on personalities. In this form of personal attack the theological intellectual has been banished to the position of a sinister undercover agent whose calling is supposedly that of sowing the seeds of unbelief *sub-rosa* within the ranks of believers.

In face of this development we need to realize that a man's ideas and plans are not necessarily suspect simply because he holds a doctor of philosophy degree. If intelligence and academic attainment automatically make the possessor's belief suspect, then Luke and Paul would fall immediately under suspicion. By the same token, a man's ideas are not necessarily wrong simply because he is not highly educated. One of the most successful pastors in the country today is a man with no formal academic degrees.

One may not like a person, a group, or an institution; that is his privilege. But to condemn the person instead of the ideas that he proclaims is not only to confuse communication but is also to participate in the practice of questionable ethics, the use of which is deplored by the world. The church cannot afford to condone a practice which when it is recognized is rejected outside of the church. At the same time there is nothing wrong with attacking a man's character if the man's character is bad.

Guilt or Innocence by Association

There are various kinds of guilt by association. There is the type of physical association of individuals which upon investigation reveals actual guilt. Criminal conspirators are not only frequently seen together but also are often guilty of both plotting and perpetrating a crime.

However, there is also a type of physical association of individuals that may not mean conspiracy or contamination. Thus in 1960 President Eisenhower deliberately arranged for a number of conferences with Nikita Khrushchev. While their meetings at Camp David and elsewhere were given a great deal of publicity, the actual topics of conversation of the two men were kept relatively secret. Yet no one except a few extremists even thought to imply that Eisenhower was stained by communistic philosophy.

Another type of guilt by association rearing its ugly head now and then has to do with association with kin. It is true, of course, that there have been enough cases of this type of guilt to lead law courts to refuse the testimony of a wife against a husband or vice versa. But this does not mean that guilt by association with kin is invariably present. One of the most embarrassing instances of this type of inferring guilt from association with kin occurred in 1955 when our own government discharged or denied commissions to several officers in our armed services because of the alleged communistic beliefs of their relatives. Fortunately, some of these officers were reinstated after public opinion forced a reversal of the decision. A popular leader in fundamentalist circles has a close relative known to be theologically liberal. However, to accuse the fundamentalist of being influenced by his relative's liberalism, or the liberal of being influenced by the fundamentalist, would be not only factually unjustifiable but also ethically dishonest.

The most frequently used form of guilt by association is that built on coincidental association. In this form two people may agree on one out of many points and thus be falsely judged to be in agreement on all points. Some of our senators favor public housing for poverty-stricken families. Communists also favor public housing. But senators who favor public housing are not communists any more than communists who favor public housing are senators. You may be opposed to segregation. Communists also are opposed to segregation. Yet this common ground of belief does not necessarily mean that you are a communist. Christ agreed with the Pharisees on such points of theology as immortality of the soul and moral responsibility; but few people would conclude from these similarities that Jesus was a Pharisee. Jesus' own scathing denunciation of the Pharisees (Matthew 23) certainly destroys such a conclusion.

Most discussion about the fallacy of association has been focused toward guilt. The opposite of the fallacy of guilt by association is also unjustified. For by the same token if one is not necessarily guilty by associations with others, neither is one necessarily innocent by his associations. Many a guilty person has tried to falsify his reputation by identifying himself with respectable friends. Perhaps the most devastating refutation of the fallacy of mere innocence by association is the example of Judas Iscariot.

The Voice of the People

Vox populi, Vox Dei — the voice of the people is the voice of God. This proverb and its inherent philosophy have had a long and stormy history. As early as the eighth century B.C. Hesiod claimed, "The voice of the people is in some ways divine."[23] Alcuin, an eighth century Christian, attacked the idea saying, "We would not listen to those who were wont to say the voice of the people is the voice of God, for the voice of the mob is near akin to madness."[24] In the sixteenth century Francis Bacon took a more mediating position: "The voice of the people has about it something divine."[25] And Alexander Pope, eighteenth century literary genius, commented on the idea in poetic form, writing:

> The people's voice is odd;
> It is, and it is not, the voice of God.[26]

Regardless of what view a person may take concerning the voice of the people, the grassroots population, the constituency, or whatever label fits best their importance cannot be discounted. Through the years appeal to the crowd has been abused until it has become marked in communication circles as a questionable procedure. Creighton defines this rhetorical device as follows: "The argumentum *ad populum* is an argument addressed to the feelings, passions, and prejudices of people rather than an unbiased discussion addressed to the intellect."[27] Frequently we hear an appeal to the crowd in political oratory. As such it may take the form of the common ground or just-plain-folks approach. An up-coming senatorial candidate, for example, may make a trip into the rural areas of his state where he describes himself as a loyal son of the soil. During his speeches in large cities, however, he may tell how as a boy he played ball in the streets, or that he too was a city kid.

---

[23]Hesiod, *Works and Days,* I. 764 (c. 735 B.C.).

[24]Alcuin, *Epistle to Charlemagne* (*Admonito ad Carolum Magnum: Works.* Epistle 127) C. 800.

[25]Francis Bacon, *De Augumentis Scientiarum,* i, 6, 89.

[26]Alexander Pope, *Imitation of Horace:* Epistles, ii, 1, 89.

[27]James Edwin Creighton, *An Introductory Logic* (New York: The Macmillan Company, 1909), p. 185.

His approach is obviously one of identification of the communicator with the common folk, the constituency.

Actually the inherent communication problem of *ad populum* does not lie in the device itself but rather in its use. Christ used the common ground approach ethically and effectively in His parables — such as those of the fishermen, the husbandman, and the shepherds. The nineteenth century preacher, Henry Ward Beecher, confessed that his sermons were failures until he studied the sermons of the apostles and found therein the key to greatness. He says:

> And I studied the sermons until I got this idea: That the Apostles were accustomed first to feel for a ground on which the people and they stood together; a common ground where they could meet. Then they heaped up a large number of the particulars of knowledge that belonged to everybody; and when they got that knowledge, which everybody would admit, placed in a proper form before their minds, then they brought it to bear upon them with all of their excited heart and feeling. That was the first definite idea of taking aim that I had in my mind.[28]

Beecher then proceeded to build a sermon on this pattern. He worked until he had assembled about forty "you all knows." Then bringing these to bear upon his audience with all his might, he succeeded in awakening seventeen men. He felt so triumphant he cried, "Now I know how to preach."[29]

Identification with the people can also be expressed in other ways such as in the cases of salesmen who want to appeal to a rich clientele and who therefore drive expensive automobiles, wear expensive clothing and adopt sophisticated airs.

Ad populum may become harmful when used to appeal

---

[28]Henry Ward Beecher, *Yale Lectures on Preaching* (New York: J. B. Ford and Company, 1872), pps. 11-12.
[29]*Ibid.*

to people's emotions rather than to their reason. The use of emotion-packed symbols identifying the speaker with the audience followed by suggestions of response to the speaker's point of view is ethical if his point of view is ethical.

Sometimes the truth which needs to be presented does not coincide with grass-roots opinion. Aristotle once said of his beloved friends and Plato, probably his teacher, ". . . while both are dear, piety requires us to honour truth above our friends."[30] Truth must be first. Communicators cannot ignore the people. As prophets of the truth of God, however, Christian communicators cannot always allow the people's wishes and dictates to control their communications. Some ministerial leaders under the supposed mandate of the people press their claims not only for generally accepted truth but also for controversial details. Their argument is that they must preach what the people demand. Yet none of these communicators would accept a church where the membership dictated what they were to preach and teach anymore than a medical doctor would take on a patient who dictated what kind of treatment he was to receive. Ministers who have been sensitive to their parishioners know how often they must present unpleasant truth no matter how unpopular the truth may be.

Our Lord was more sensitive to the masses than any other who has ever lived. His love for them is shown in Matthew: "But when he saw the multitudes, he was moved with compassion on them, because they fainted, and were scattered abroad, as sheep having no shepherd" (Matthew 9: 36). Yet for all of His compassion He refused to conform His message to their demands. He could speak in the people's tongue and sway the masses, but never did He compromise the truth He was sent to bring. Even during His last hours He became a victim of the people. He was cruci-

---

[30]Aristotle, *Nicomachean Ethics,* I, 6, 1.

fied as a result of a crude and cruel *ad populum*. The voice of the people said, "Crucify him" (Mark 15:13).

From His life and ministry comes the pattern to follow: always be sensitive to the people and never to stoop to un-ethical *ad populum*. Always set forth the truth to meet the people's varied needs. Never must we be frightened into a compromise of the truth. The task is sharply defined by Alexander Pushkin in "The Prophet":

> Arise, oh, prophet, watch and hearken
> And with my Will thy soul engird.
> Roam the grey seas, the roads that darken
> And burn men's hearts with this my Word.[31]

Clouding the Issue

Communicators may cloud an issue in a number of ways.

Equivocation occurs when a speaker shifts the meaning of a term within a context. In modern parlance equivoca-tion is sometimes called double talk. For example, the term equality is a high-order abstraction which may have one meaning in a certain context and a different meaning in another context. When used in the context of our Declara-tion of Independence to refer to man's equal rights to life, liberty, and the pursuit of happiness, equality may be justi-fiably defended. When equality is used in terms of man's physical characteristics, social status, or intellectual endow-ments, it may be easily refuted. Equivocation occurs when a speaker in attacking the idea of the equality of man's rights as defined in our Declaration of Independence uses the term equality in the sense of equal physical character-istics, social status, or intellectual endowments.

In theological circles the fallacy of equivocation easily goes unnoticed because theological terms are highly ab-

---

[31]Alexander Pushkin, "The Prophet" in *The Poems, Prose and Plays of Alexander Pushkin* ed. Avrahm Yarmolinsky (New York: The Modern Library, Random House, Inc., 1936), p. 62.

stract. The term inspiration of the scriptures has different meanings to different men. To some inspiration means that God literally dictated every word of each book of the Bible to the writers whose names they bear. To another inspiration means that the Holy Spirit prompted each writer, allowing him to write in his own style but protecting him from error. To yet another theologian inspiration means that Bible writers were merely stimulated more highly than other men and thus recorded elevated ideas. No one can deny that these and other meanings of the term inspiration are in use today. Equivocation occurs when a speaker shifts the meaning of the term deliberately for ulterior motives. When on one occasion a man uses the term inspiration to identify himself with orthodoxy, and on another occasion to identify himself with liberalism, he is guilty of equivocation.

Communicators can learn to detect equivocation by training themselves to analyze the key words in any statement. Pick out all words in the statement which may have more than one meaning. Try to determine which meaning a speaker or writer is using. Analyze the total context of a given message to determine whether key words are used consistently or equivocally. Keep in mind that shifts in meaning are relatively easy to detect within one statement but difficult to detect within a longer discourse. Challenge the fallacy of equivocation whenever possible. Try to avoid equivocation by critically evaluating your own messages, for nothing is ever gained by either innocent or contrived equivocation.

Amphiboly refers to fallacy caused by faulty grammatical construction. A statement may lack clarity because of the loose or awkward way in which the words are put together. Frequently amphiboly is not only misleading but ludicrous. For example, some will recall the World War II posters which urged us to "Save soap and waste paper." *The Reader's Digest* reported several humorous journalistic slips, such as that taken from a TV previews column on the program "The Eleventh Hour" which said, "This is the first episode of a series which will bring you one full hour of mental illness every week," and from the Jackson *Floridian*: "Honorable mentions in the school science fair were Tim Culbertson with the anatomy of a chicken, and Robert Frank with the nervous system of an earthworm."[32] One of the most amusing series of amphibolies gathered together at one time was reported by George W. Feinstein of Pasadena City College in a purported letter from a former student:

> Dear sir; you never past me in grammer because you was prejudice but I got this here athaletic scholarship any way. Well, the other day I finely get to writing the rule's down so as I can always study it if they ever slip my mind.
>
> 1. Each pronoun agrees with their antecedent.
> 2. Just between you and I, case is important.
> 3. Verbs has to agree with their subjects.
> 4. Watch out for irregular verbs which has crope into our language.
> 5. Don't use no double negatives.
> 6. A writer mustn't shift your point of view.
> 7. When dangling, don't use participles.
> 8. Join clauses good, like a conjunction should.
> 9. Don't write a run-on sentence you got to punctuate it.
> 10. About sentence fragments.
> 11. In letters themes reports articles and stuff like that we use commas to keep a string of items apart.
> 12. Don't use commas, which aren't necessary.
> 13. Its important to use apostrophe's right.
> 14. Don't abbrev.
> 15. Check to see if you any words out.
> 16. In my opinion I think that an author when he is writing shouldn't get into the habit of making use of too many unnecessary words that he does not really need in order to put his message across.
> 17. In the case of a business letter, check it in terms of jargon.
> 18. About repetition, the repetition of a word might be real effective repetition — take, for instance, Abraham Lincoln.

---

[32]From "Pardon, Your Slip is Showing," *The Reader's Digest*, LXXXII, (March, 1963), 119.

19. As far as incomplete constructions, they are wrong.
20. Last but not least, lay off cliches.[33]

Seriously, however, amphibolies are not really humorous, and as they only confuse communication, they should be avoided. The communicator must not only speak and write so others can understand him, he must speak and write so others cannot misunderstand him. Faulty grammatical constructions in the communication messages reduce clarity and mar the communicator's image giving the impression that he is unlearned or incapable of communicating clearly.

Accent is a fallacy caused by emphasizing the wrong word or idea in discourse. Accent is usually more apparent in oral than in written communication although it occurs in both. Notice how the location of accent may change the meaning of the old proverb:

> Woman without her man would be lost.
> Woman, without her, man would be lost.

Accent may extend beyond the words of a sentence. Thoughts, sentences, and even whole paragraphs may be removed from their contexts and by improper emphasis be distorted. For example, one could make a seemingly strong case for hedonism[34] by removing the following Biblical verse from its context and citing it as support for such a philosophy:

> There is nothing better for a man, than that he should eat and drink, and find enjoyment in his toil. This also, I saw, is from the hand of God (Ecclesiastes 2:24 RSV).

Thus not only is the Bible cited in support of seeming fleshly indulgences, but God is shown to be the provider of

---

[33]George W. Feinstein, "Letter from A Triple-Threat Grammarian," *College English*, XXI (April, 1960), 408. Reprinted with the permission of the National Council of Teachers of English and George W. Feinstein.

[34]The teaching that pleasure or happiness is the only or chief good in life.

such living. However, when one adds to the above verse the remaining words and thoughts of the verse's rightful context, quite a different philosophy emerges. Thus the author of Ecclesiastes continues,

> For apart from him who can eat or who can have enjoyment? For to the man who pleases him God gives wisdom and knowledge and joy; but to the sinner he gives the work of gathering and heaping, only to give to one who pleases God. This also is vanity and a striving after wind (Ecclesiastes 2:25-26 RSV).

The remainder of the context makes God the end and object of all the activities of life.

Faulty punctuation contributes to faulty accent. The King James version of the Bible renders Psalm 121:1-2 as follows:

> I will lift up mine eyes unto the hills, from whence cometh my help. My help cometh from the Lord, which made heaven and earth.

The punctuation in the above quotation has caused some observers to think that the psalmist's help came from the inspiration he received in viewing majestic mountains. The Revised Standard Version has probably come closer to the correct punctuation and translation of the thought rendering it as follows:

> I lift up my eyes to the hills.
> From whence does my help come?
> My help comes from the Lord,
> Who made heaven and earth (Psalm 121:1-2 RSV).

Here the punctuation actually clarifies the thought and accents the correct ideas.

Faulty accent frequently occurs in verbal communication. By vocally emphasizing certain words or ideas and de-emphasizing others, a speaker points up the idea he considers most important. Accenting wrong ideas or words obviously will confuse the issue.

The practice of incorrectly emphasizing another man's vocal or written ideas is equally serious. It is unethical to take portions of another's speech or writings out of their context and make these portions mean something quite different from what the original author intended. Such distortion of accent is considered to be out of bounds in all communication circles. A high degree of sensitivity to the truth must be developed so that truth will never be distorted.

Ooerverbalization, sometimes called loquacity or verbiage, frequently blocks communication. Oververbalization, like amphiboly, has its amusing as well as its serious side. Halford Luccock tells the conversation of a man speaking to another man dying of thirst in the Sahara:

> Let us consider the properties of what we call water. Water is a colorless liquid which on being raised to a temperature of a hundred degrees centigrade or two-hundred and twelve degrees Fahrenheit, becomes what is called vapour. If, hov.ever, on the other hand, the temperature is lowered to no degrees Centigrade, or thirty-two degrees Fahrenheit, lo, it is ice! In the final analysis it is discovered to consist of two portions of hydrogen to one of oxygen, hence arises the name H_2O. The thirsty man interrupts, "For the love of God, mister, a drink!"[35]

On the serious side, however, extreme over-verbalization may indicate some kind of personality maladjustment. Some people talk too much for various reasons. Some are verbose because they find silence embarrassing or disturbing. Most of us at one time or another have found ourselves entertaining an underverbalized individual or party. Because we have little in common, conversation comes hard, and we search for topics to discuss. We perhaps need to learn that silence in social gatherings is not necessarily evil, and it may be decidedly beneficial. Others talk incessantly to cover up a sense of inferiority or insecurity. Lack of edu-

---

[35]Halford E. Luccock, *Communicating the Gospel* (New York: Harper & Brothers, Publishers, 1954), p. 128.

cation and social acceptance have figured heavily in the lives of some gossips who spend hours on the telephone. Some Christians evidently feel a sense of security and possibly superiority in everlastingly possessing the latest news to pass around to uninformed church members.

Unfortunately, certain individuals use over-verbalization for the questionable purpose of evasion. Some politicians evade committing themselves on vital issues not by silence but by talking long and loudly without ever getting to their real positions. The use of verbiage or abstract terminology to bury a communicator's meaning is obviously unethical and certainly unsound if done unconsciously.

Some men seem to speak and write with heavy verbiage to impress others with their grasp of academic terminology or with their large vocabulary. Scholars often argue that technical terminology is necessary to cover detailed ideas which would otherwise demand many words for explanation. Such an assertion is true to some degree, but the argument is overdone. Most disciplines have developed an immense and often baffling glossary of technical terms understood only by the initiated. The physical and medical scientists' jargon is all but meaningless to the outsider. Religious and theological terminology is distressingly abstract and meaningless to the untrained. Even the communication vocabulary is often unintelligible to the individual who knows nothing of semantics, cybernetics, or rhetoric. As for philosophical terminology, Will Durant has this to say,

> But we "moderns" have become so accustomed to windy verbiage in philosophy that when philosophy is presented without the verbiage we can with difficulty recognize it. One must pay a penalty for having a prejudice against obscurity.[36]

---

[36]Will Durant, *The Story of Philosophy the Lives and Opinions of the Greater Philosophers* (New York: Pocket Books, Inc., 1954), p. xiii.

These observations may be an oversimplification of a difficult communication problem, but study of the writings in various fields leaves the distinct impression that the truths contained therein could be presented much more concisely and clearly in many cases. Would scholars lose academic caste if they talked and wrote so people could understand them? As for the church, the apostle Paul in discussing the problem of speaking in tongues in the Corinthian church sounded a warning which is relevant to all of us:

> If even lifeless instruments, such as the flute or the harp, do not give distinct notes, how will anyone know what is played? And if the bugle gives an indistinct sound, who will get ready for battle? So with yourselves; if you in a tongue utter speech that is not intelligible, how will anyone know what is said? For you will be speaking into the air (I Corinthians 14:7-9 RSV).

Underverbalization, or taciturnity when seen in shy and quiet persons may create a barrier to communication. It may also be an indication of some personality maladjustment when present in the extreme. Feelings of inferiority or guilt may account for a quietness tinged with fear. Some underverbalized people have desperately tried to communicate with others, but because the intended receivers have ignored or out-talked them, they have withdrawn. Some individuals hesitate to talk or write unless they can put their thoughts in precisely correct words, as though there were one and only one way to state an idea. An understanding of the many uses of words could alleviate such hesitation. Inordinate fear of conversation may suggest serious anti-social or other emotional states which should be treated by professional counselors. Speech pathologists, psychologists, and psychiatrists are equipped to analyze and help those who are handicapped in serious ways.

Thus it is possible for communication to be broken in many ways. Emotional outbursts, the appeal to tradition, the pointing to another wrong, humor and ridicule, demand for special consideration, and many other irrelevancies can block the flow of ideas between people. Christians must work untiringly to remove all such barriers. No individual or institution has a greater stake in the human communication process than the Christian and the church. Accordingly, we need to adopt as our own the testimony of Paul and his co-workers when they said:

Therefore, being engaged in this service by the mercy of God, we do not lose heart. We have renounced disgraceful, underhanded ways; we refuse to practice cunning or to tamper with God's word, but by the open statement of the truth we would commend ourselves to every man's conscience in the sight of God. And even if our gospel is veiled, it is veiled only to those who are perishing. In their case the god of this world has blinded the minds of the unbelievers, to keep them from seeing the light of the gospel of the glory of Christ, who is the likeness of God. For what we preach is not ourselves, but Jesus Christ as Lord, with ourselves as your servants for Jesus' sake. For it is the God who said, "Let light shine out of darkness," who has shone in our hearts to give the light of the knowledge of the glory of God in the face of Christ.

(II Corinthians 4:1-6 RSV).

Chapter Five

Group Communication

No man should be always alone. He should not be alone in his church life or in his personal life. A life lived in splendid isolation may give an impression of rugged individualism but such a life cannot accurately portray true Christian purpose. The writer to the Hebrews seeing the disintegrative effects of isolationism in the early church wrote:

> And let us consider how to stir up one another to love and good works, not neglecting to meet together, as is the habit of some, but encouraging one another, and all the more as you see the Day drawing near (Hebrews 10:24-25 RSV).

The basic need and urge for being together, for membership in a community, for participation in a group form the foundation of the *koinonia*, the Christian community. The Greek word *koinonia* in its original form meant common, and it was used in connection with business partnerships

148

or of the owning of shares in something with someone. Ultimately in Christian circles *koinonia* came to mean fellowship or communion.[1] For the early Christians held something in common — to them this community property was the church.

In this present day it is a strange paradox that in spite of Christians' longing to be part of the Christian community, one of the most serious communication breakdowns is at this community level made up of the local church. Almost every denomination is plagued with such community breakdown. Church splits send individuals and groups careening off in every direction. Some of these drift into different churches, some into cults, and some away from the church altogether.

Many of the factors of group communication relate equally to the universal church as well as to the local church. Churches are communication centers. As such communication centers their major function is sharing — sharing the Gospel, sharing life, and sharing fellowship. Churches must not become introverted communities catering only to the initiated and perpetuating their private exclusivism which even includes their own jargon.

A local church should relate to individuals, to its surrounding community, to the universal church, and to the world. The wider the circle of these relationships, the more complex becomes the local church's communication task. Though we know group relationships progress geometrically and not simply additively, the increasing complexity must not deter the local church from continuing its efforts to communicate. Healthy local churches contribute to the health of the larger Christian fellowship. To avoid disintegration, introversion, and the resulting communication

---

[1] G. Abbott-Smith, *A Manual Greek Lexicon of the New Testament* (third edition, Edinburgh: T. & T. Clark, 1937), pp. 250-51.

failure, a fresh look needs to be taken at the local church — its nature, condition, and renewal.

I

THE NATURE OF THE CHURCH AS A GROUP

The church is usually defined theologically in terms of both its universal and local aspects. Because of the increased interest in ecumenicity these theological definitions are becoming more important than ever. Theological bearings can be taken from the Biblical doctrine of the church, the broad outlines of which are sketched by Paul in his first letter to the Corinthians saying, "Unto the church of God which is at Corinth, to them that are sanctified in Christ Jesus, called to be saints, with all that in every place call upon the name of Jesus Christ our Lord, both theirs and ours" (I Corinthians 1:2). Such guidelines steer away from extreme or lopsided emphasis either on broad ecclesiasticism or on narrow sectarianism. The church, according to Paul's inspired words, is both local and universal.

The local church involves most Christians more intimately than the universal church. The dynamics of smaller church groups, of course, have both similarities with and differences from the larger groups. Nevertheless many of the principles of communication in a small group carry over to communication in a larger group.

Definitions of the local church vary according to denominational tradition and Biblical interpretation. Most definitions are found in the heady air of theological abstraction. For example, Baptists have for years been taught that,

> A Christian Church is a company of regenerate persons, baptized on a profession of faith in Christ; united in covenant for worship, instruction, the observance of Christian ordinances, and for such service as the Gospel requires; recognizing and accepting Christ as their supreme Lord and lawgiver, and taking His

Word as their only and sufficient rule of faith and practice in all matters of conscience and religion.[2]

Such a definition can be helpful as a general guideline for local church government and instruction. However, a gap exists between the idealism of the definition and the realism of the functioning of the average church. What is a church *really* like? What is the practical, not the theological, nature of the local church? The local church group is ordinarily thought of as a collection of people of various ages, sexes, and socio-economic levels gathered together on a Sunday morning for the sermon which has traditionally been a one-way communication affair of greater or lesser influence. This type of meeting certainly has enduring value. Nevertheless, consider the many other gatherings of the church during the week. Here smaller face-to-face groups meet. Here church members exchange ideas, consider business, and make policy decisions. Informal pockets of fellowship and friendship are created, and it is possible subtly to influence and persuade others either to join or drift away.

Small groups such as the local church's monthly board meetings exhibit more concrete and revealing characteristics than the average theological description provides. S. R. Slavson describes a small group as,

> . . . an aggregation of three or more persons in an informal face-to-face relation where there is direct and dynamic interaction among the individuals comprising it, and as a result the personality of each member is fundamentally modified.[3]

There is a difference between a collection of people and an organized group. A half dozen or more neighbors may

---

[2]Edward T. Hiscox, *The New Directory for Baptist Churches* (Philadelphia: The Judson Press, 1894), p. 20. Used by permission.

[3]S. R. Slavson, *An Introduction to Group Therapy* (New York: International Universities Press, 1943), p. 21.

drift together into a backyard, decide to have a cup of coffee, and spend the evening talking and laughing together. Each participant in this case may tell of incidents in his own life or argue his own political or religious point of view. The men may discuss baseball, taxes, or international affairs. The women may cluster together by themselves and discuss children, schools, or fashions. Such a gathering as this would hardly be called an organized group even though all may be on the same patio.

In contrast to such a haphazard group or collection, consider a church nominating committee. Made up of a half dozen men and women who meet regularly to select leaders and officers for their church, the committee has a list of offices to fill and a procedure for filling them. It continues to function until all officers have been chosen and elected. What are the specific differences between the two groups described above? What makes one just a collection of people and the other an organized group?

Although both may loosely be described as groups containing individuals who interact with and influence one another, the nominating committee shows distinct differences from the neighborhood gathering. The nominating committee is conscious of being an organized group, has a specific and relatively stable membership, has a common purpose and set of goals, reveals interdependence of participants for group and task efficiency, and has a high degree of successful communication between all members. The neighborhood gathering does not think of itself as an organized group; its participants may change from time to time, or it may disband altogether; it has no specific purpose or goals other than a desire for a friendly meeting; it has little consciousness of interdependence; and its communication process may exclude certain members of the gathering.

There are many other characteristics of groups which are not mentioned above. Students of group dynamics talk about such additional group factors as skill in performance, reward, sense of belonging, individual and group balance, morale, group background, cohesion, and standards. All of these forces are at work in a constantly changing group situation. The characteristics of groups describe a church group as well as a secular group. The study of group characteristics indicates that there are two important factors about a group in the study of group communication — the personnel of groups and the functions of groups.

The Personnel of the Group

A group's philosophy of operation often determines the nature of its personnel and *vice versa*. Some people join a certain church group because of its autocratic government, for in such a group they are spared the burden of making decisions. The built-in leadership of an autocratic organization takes care of planning, programming, and propagandizing its sole point of view, and the members merely go along with superimposed plans. Others may join a church where the leadership is weak, and a virtual anarchy exists. In this type of situation every member of the group does what is right in his own eyes, and the indulgence of self-expression is the privilege of every individualist. Still others may join a church because it provides a democratic type of government where they may participate in the goal-setting, policy-making, and program planning activities of the group without swinging too far either toward autocracy or anarchy.

Each of these types of groups can function to a greater or lesser degree of efficiency, but they are at their greatest efficiency in a democratic framework. The classic experiment of Lewin and Lippitt in the 1930's supports this statement.[4] The purpose of their project was to measure the

---

[4]Kurt Lewin and Ronald Lippitt, "An Experimental Approach to the Study of Autocracy and Democracy: A Preliminary Note," *Sociometry A Journal of Interpersonal Relations, I* (January-April, 1938), 292-300.

effects of different types of leadership behavior on boys divided into groups for the experiment. The three types of leadership measured were *laissez-faire* groups in which complete freedom for group or individual decision making existed, and a minimum of leader participation was exercised; *autocratic,* or *authoritarian* led groups in which the leader determined all policies and details; and *democratically* led groups in which all policies and details were discussed, criticisms were invited, and decisions were made by the group with encouragement and assistance of the leader. The results of the experiment were varied, but in general the researchers discovered that as they improved in learning the democratically led groups were superior in such matters as motivation, satisfaction, friendliness, teamwork, and increase in productivity. Authoritarian or autocratically led groups were superior in amount of work produced in a short time but encountered more hostility, competition, aggression, and dependence in the group. The *laissez-faire* groups appeared to be the least effective. Both the quality and quantity of their work was inferior, for they wasted more time and talked more about their work. The *laissez-faire* groups also experienced more aggression among themselves than the democratic groups but less than the autocratically led groups. It must be pointed out that research subsequent to the experiments of Lewin and Lippitt would support the idea that certain situations call for authoritarian and others for *laissez-faire* leadership. Advantages and disadvantages are inherent in each of the types of group atmosphere, but the democratic approach seems to offer the most possibilities for a healthy church group. Situations calling for authoritarian or *laissez-faire* do not parallel church life where democratic leadership seems to produce more satisfactory results.[5] Church groups have

---

[5]Harold Guetzkow, *Groups, Leadership and Men* (Pittsburgh: Carnegie Press, 1951).

prospered under all three types of organization, but some kind of democratic approach that does not eliminate pastoral leadership would seem to be most ideal.

In any group situation the personnel are involved in what is called role-playing, and this practice may take different forms. Role-playing is the practice of one person acting the life of another; for example, a child assuming the role of a fireman or pilot. There are constructive group roles and destructive group roles. D. M. Hall describes constructive group roles as those of the orienter, the facilitator, the encourager-harmonizer, the recorder, and the observer.[6] The destructive group roles he lists are the aggressor-dominator, the censor-blocker, the blamer-dodger, the submisser, the isolate, and the dependent.[7] Each role's title is descriptive of its action.

A pastor who has worked for any length of time with church groups will recognize the above-listed types. He encounters some church builders. He is confronted with some church destroyers. Obviously the pastor and church group as a whole have no difficulty with the builders. It should be equally obvious, then, that the task in the group is not just to set goals, plan programs, and make decisions. The task is also to solve problems, the greatest of which may be caused by the group destroying individuals within. Individual and group therapy is of paramount importance here. The improvement of communication within the group is mandatory if communication with those outside the group is to be accomplished.

The Functions of the Group

Many local churches scarcely know why they exist. A

---

[6]D. M. Hall, *Dynamics of Group Action* (Danville, Illinois: Interstate Printers and Publishers, Inc., 1957), p. 19.
[7]*Ibid.*, pp. 2-23.

definition of goals and an effort at attaining these goals would surely increase the local church's capabilities. Two broad goals of group life are important to the church — one is fellowship and the other is service.

The fellowship function of the church. Most people crave group fellowship, the feeling of being accepted by and belonging to a group. In secular activity the craving for fellowship can be observed in such gatherings as the bridge circle or the coffee gang. This craving, called also gregariousness or the herd instinct, is one of man's many complex drives or motivations. Consequently, gregariousness is one of the reasons some people go to church. If this seemingly simple factor were all there were to the church-going situation, the suggested procedure would appear to be equally simple; the churches could heighten their fellowship activities and be crowded every service. Unfortunately, the problem is much more complex. What are the sociometric[8] problems the church faces?

The problem of friendship selectivity is a major one. Early in life individuals begin to show selective preference in their friendships. This selectivity depends upon such things as response or indifference between people. We tend to like those who respond to us and dislike those who ignore or even repulse us. In the church situation such selectivity is normally acceptable; indeed it is helpful. This principle of selectivity has won countless people into the church. Most people were initially led to their first church experience by an individual who cared enough for them to go out of his way to bring them to church and to befriend them while they were there.

Selectivity, however, grows within an individual in terms of his inherent preferences. Lois B. Murphy experimented

---

[8]Sociometry is a study of the social aspects of group life with specific focus on the emotional quality of the interpersonal relationships among group members.

extensively with selectivity and discovered that the whole psychological field plays a direct role in determining the kind of selectivity behavior involved. Thus, the presence or absence of every social and physical element within a person's experience has its influence on his choices.[9]

This brings us to another consideration for group fellowship in the local church. How are the friendship selectivities working out? Are they developing an integrated or a fragmented group? If a group's integration is poor, then the conditions for effective communication are also poor. The converse of this is equally true: if integration is good, communication is likely to be good. Unfortunately, many church groups labor under the delusion that their integration is satisfactory when actually it is not. Even in large and apparently successful churches cliques and social groups which are difficult or impossible for an outsider to penetrate are frequently present. How can one discover the social pattern of a church group?

J. L. Moreno and Helen Jennings have experimented extensively and effectively with the discovery of social patterns. Moreno devised a sociometric test which allowed individuals in groups to test their own group social patterns.[10] The test was a simple yet highly productive one. It merely asked each individual in a school classroom to write down secretly on a piece of paper the two individuals in the classroom they would prefer to have sit on either side of them the next term; they were to rank them in the order of their preference. The simplicity of the test plus its lack of resemblance to a test in the minds of the individuals participating made it highly successful. It allowed the experi-

---

[9]Lois B. Murphy, *Social Behavior and Child Personality* (New York: Columbia University Press, 1937).

[10]J. L. Moreno, *Who Shall Survive? A New Approach to the Problem of Human Interrelations.* Collaborator: Helen H. Jennings (Washington: Nervous and Mental Diseases Publishing Co., 1934), p. 13.

menters to determine the structure of the group and the actual network of relationships which existed. This meant that a reorganization of the group and its function could proceed if necessary.

Such a test applied to a local church could provide similar successful results. The health of the congregation as a **group** could be analyzed. If individuals in the group were **asked** to list the names of three or more within the group with whom they would like to serve on a committee, accompany to a rally, or entertain in their homes, the results could possibly reveal the group's health. If, for example, in a youth group numbering ten each member was chosen at least twice and no one individual more than four times, the group would appear to be well integrated and healthy. If, on the other hand, of that same group and number, one or two were chosen nine times and one or more not chosen at all, the group would appear to be non-integrated and of questionable health. A non-integrated group would be characterized by cliquishness and exclusivism, and the leader of such a group ought to be watching for symptoms of interpersonal blockages, distortions, and communication breakdowns within the group.

Cliquishness is caused by misevaluations on the part of the individuals involved. Misevaluations leading to cliquishness may be caused by ignorance of or complacency toward group issues and goals. Such ignorance or complacency indicates that the members of the clique are out of touch with the realities of their environment. Causes of misevaluation are extremism on the part of individuals who either want nothing changed or who want everything changed and allness attitudes expressed in rigid, absolutistic terms indicating that the individuals involved know all about the situation or that they always have the last word on a problem.

When such danger signs are found in a church, their seriousness must be determined. They indicate not only poor group communication and poor group health, but they invariably point to individual problems. Extreme egocentricity, fear, jealousy, lack of sympathy for others, poor judgment and other maladjustments may be some of the individual problems. To the Christian such problems suggest a lack of the fruits of the Spirit and the presence of the works of the flesh (Galatians 5:17-26). In advanced forms persons involved in a group with such problems may develop not herd instinct but herd fear. Integrating these persons adequately into the group becomes an important objective.

The service function of the church. Fellowship, even on a high level, is not enough to keep a group intact. There must be goals to attain, objectives to pursue, and services to perform. Most of us at one time or another have been members of a group that seemed to get nowhere. Although the mere setting of goals does not insure their realization or the consequent effectiveness of the group, it is equally true that the group which is heading nowhere will doubtless arrive there. There are many factors necessary to group effectiveness. They exist in various degrees of importance. The following list is not exhaustive but fairly representative.

1. Clarity of goals
2. Agreement on major and minor goals
3. Agreement on methods of attaining the goals
4. Support of group activities
5. Coordination of activities in group tasks
6. Availability of resources necessary for task accomplishment (intellectual, economic, etc.)
7. Effectiveness of communication
8. Competence of leadership
9. Clarity of lines of authority
10. Participation in decisions.[11]

This list may be used as a general standard by which to measure the effectiveness of most church groups. Goals and functions are closely intertwined. They should be

---

[11]See on this Dorwin Cartwright and Alvin Zander, (ed.) *Group Dynamics Research and Theory* (second edition; New York: Row, Peterson and Company, 1960), pp. 345 ff.

planned and carried out in terms of the church's immediate, short-range, and long-range objectives.

Goals and functions in the church will vary according to the church's size and philosophy. Each church should evaluate itself, its effectiveness, its goals, and its functions; and the entire group should be involved in any resulting decisions. Writings in the fields of pastoral theology, church management, and evangelism suggest the church's goals and methods and should be consulted as guidelines.[12] Goals and methods ought to be worked out in detail under the following categories: evangelism, missions, Christian education, Christian social life, spiritual culture, cultivation of harmony and unity within the church, community tasks, and denominational and interdenominational responsibilities.

When a church group sincerely and realistically evaluates itself in terms of such goals and functions, it is likely to prosper. Failure to so evaluate itself may only perpetuate a church's ineffectiveness.

II

THE CONDITION OF THE CHURCH GROUP

A group like an individual, may become sick. A group may also evade treatment for so long that drastic measures

---

[12]See for example Andrew Blackwood, *Pastoral Leadership* (New York: Abingdon-Cokesbury Press, 1949), pp. 16-24; William H. Leach, *Handbook of Church Management* (Englewood Cliffs, N. J.: Prentice-Hall Inc., 1958), pp. 18-23; Gaines S. Dobbins, *Building Better Churches, A Guide to the Pastoral Ministry* (Nashville, Tennessee: Broadman Press, 1947), pp. 18-28; Lloyd M. Perry, and Edward J. Lias, *A Manual of Pastoral Problems and Procedures* (Grand Rapids, Michigan: Baker Book House, 1962), p. 1; Alvin J. Lindgren, *Foundations for Purposeful Church Administration* (New York: Abingdon Press, 1965); Faris D. Whitesell, *Basic New Testament Evangelism* (Grand Rapids, Michigan: Zondervan Publishing House, 1949); George E. Sweazey, *Effective Evangelism The Greatest Work in the World* (New York: Harper and Brothers, Publishers, 1953); and others.

may be needed to remedy the problem. The early church was threatened by the deceit of Ananias and Sapphira, and their deaths had a sobering effect upon the whole church (Acts 5:1-11). Paul's treatment of the offender in the church at Corinth illustrates the seriousness with which early Christian leaders approached the problem of discipline (I Corinthians 5). Subsequently less drastic measures of problem-solving and discipline were used, but the health of the total church body was never neglected.

A group, like an individual, can also be healthy. The early church in spite of certain problems was unusually robust. In spite of discouraging persecution it went about vigorously preaching the Gospel, and some of its leaders were so effective that they were accused of turning the world upside down (Acts 17:6).

A church is seldom completely healthy or completely sick. Nevertheless, it can be predominantly one way or the other, and alert Christians will constantly be on the lookout for those symptoms of health or sickness which point to the condition of their church body.

Group Atmosphere: Open or Closed?

The Western World thinks of the modern Communist nations as unhealthy because of the closed and inhibited atmosphere which hangs over them. Iron curtains and Berlin walls stifle liberty. Freedom of thought, speech, and travel are all closely curtailed. Earl Wiley tells of the man who talked himself to death in three words. He shouted, "Down with Stalin!"[13] A similar statement in China today using the names of contemporary leaders would very probably have similar results.

A church group is certainly unhealthy if it reveals such

---

[13]Earl W. Wiley, "The Enthymeme: Idiom of Persuasion," *The Quarterly Journal of Speech*, XLII (February, 1956), 19.

symptoms as authoritarianism, oligarchy, autocracy, and dictatorship. Such an atmosphere precludes the participation of all members in planning or problem solving. Ultimately such an atmosphere will rob members of their incentive to work or to shoulder responsibility. They will not care.

The democratic nature of the New Testament church implies participation. When one individual or even a small group does all the planning and problem solving, they face the danger of either resentment or apathy; and the poor cooperation of the rest of the members is assured.

The closed-minded group is often characterized by the attitude of intensionality which means words become more important than facts. Allness thinking predominates, and leaders within the group are convinced that they are the sole guardians of the truth. Individual members in such an atmosphere feel secure within the environs of the group, and outsiders are the enemy. Pressed to its extreme this type of group has been known to explode in vicious fanaticism which may even operate in the name of Christianity brushing love and ethics aside in an insane fight for the preservation of what it calls the truth.

How refreshingly healthy is the church which rejects such attitudes. Carrying out its work fearlessly, this church maintains openness of mind and freedom of participation. It is extensionally oriented and constantly seeks to know the facts in any given situation. It seldom claims to know all there is to know about problems and after thorough investigation of any area of plan or conflict, keeps its mind open, ready for further discovery or possible adjustment. Such an atmosphere makes for a healthy church.

Group Self-evaluation: Willing or Unwilling?

A second sign of group health or sickness has to do with the willingness of the group to evaluate itself. No group is immune to deterioration, and the only deterrent to group deterioration is constant vigil and critical self-evaluation. A church group may fail to set up a system for feedback, or it may fail to sense the feedback already existing in its membership. It may deliberately ignore the danger signals fed back to it from many sources. If the group fails at any of these points of self-evaluation, its health may be impaired.

Unrealistic views of the organization. A happy balance in our views of life is difficult to keep regardless of what we are considering. And it is difficult to maintain a balanced view of our church. We may think of our church as a sort of heirloom or the main piece of furniture in our family's collection for many generations. Or, because a church has become a new and thrilling experience in an otherwise drab life, it may be thought of as holy ground. Either way the church can be overrated as a result. When the church is thought of as an heirloom or as holy ground, the group cannot be wrong. The church has done things a certain way for generations and cannot be changed; no individual will be allowed to come in and upset years of experience. The church becomes a sacred cow with no faults or weaknesses, and individuals get lost in a mob.

Underrating the group is as bad as overrating it. In underrating members tend to deride the organization by innuendo and sarcasm. Behind-the-back gossip and criticism rob a church of effectiveness. In this type of situation the group can do no right, and individualism may develop into anarchy which is just as unhealthy as mob rule.

Unrealistic views of the personnel. Unrealistic attitudes within the group are often projected toward its personnel. The problems of overevaluation or underevaluation may take place. In such a situation where overevaluation exists, leaders may be overrated. Their personalities, political maneuvering, and other factors may well distract attention from their abilities or lack of same. Sometimes such personnel have to be replaced, and replacement requires the utmost in tact and love. Many replacement problems can be avoided by wise selections of leaders in the first place.

The underrating of personnel appears to have less complications for the group than it has for the individuals involved. The group will certainly profit in the long run if the most competent personnel available is used in leadership positions. Furthermore, few groups can afford to suffer the loss of unused talent, a danger resulting from underrating.

Unrealistic view of goals. Group goals often run the risk of being unrealistic and thus are prone to failure unless the group as a whole contributes to the formulation and realization of its goals. All members should feel commitment to the same goals to avoid either partial cooperation or continuous friction. The half-hearted support of unwanted goals will sap the strength of a church and may lead to divisive subgroups. Failure of the total group to formulate and support its goals may result in these goals being unrealistic in several ways.

The adoption of goals beyond the abilities and desires of the group is not only unrealistic but is symptomatic of group illness. Sunday school membership totals, evangelistic objectives, financial budgets, building plans, and other service goals can be set out of all reasonable reach. For years one pastor and one church prided themselves on planning and carrying a church budget of which half went for current expenses and half for missions. This budget made good publicity for the church. However, the actual current expense portion of the church's income, though half of the total, could only provide for part of the minister's salary. As a result the minister was forced to spend much of his time in secular employment to provide for his family's needs. Thus in reality the pastor himself supplemented the current expense side of the budget disproportionately to the remainder of the membership, for the fifty-fifty budget figure was in reality a myth. Under such circumstances normal numerical growth and spiritual progress of a church is undoubtedly retarded.

A church group can also underset its goals. Undersetting goals occurs more often than oversetting them. Many churches reveal their immaturity and spiritual illness by overly conservative goal setting. The undersetting of goals can take place in virtually every area of the church's program. Mission programs, evangelism, church extension, giving, and many other worthy projects can suffer from this tragic lack of vision.

The clinging to outdated goals whether these goals are too large or too small is a telltale symptom of group illness. A classic illustration of this problem of outdated goals is seen in the development of the group worship structure used by the Judeo-Christian religion. First came the tabernacle and when its function became obsolete, it gave way to the temple. The temple in turn gradually faded in importance and was superseded by the synagogue as new goals and objectives became necessary. Ultimately in the providence of God the synagogue failed in its usefulness to the people when the very nature, demands, and goals of Christianity called for a revised structure. This new structure became known as the church. The basic structure of the church is pliable enough to make it adequate for ministering to man's needs as long as he is willing to evaluate its strengths and weaknesses. This evaluation will have to be carried out in the light of new goals. Realistic views of our church organization, its personnel, and its goals must be cultivated. When such evaluation continually takes place, our churches will be healthy.

Group Responsibility: Accepted or Rejected?

The churches have always deplored their inability to challenge all of their adherents to lives of responsibility. Continually challenging the membership to live responsibly is one of the minister's biggest problems. The problem of responsible living is not isolated to church groups. It is distressingly present in almost every group. Industrial unions, neighborhood clubs, school organizations, volunteer agencies, and virtually every other type of aggregation lament the lack of group and individual participation. They all recognize that nonparticipation contributes to the sickness of the group.

If participation within a group promotes health, lack of participation certainly indicates some type of group illness. In the church body as in the human body each individual organism must fulfill its responsibility and function or the whole will suffer. Even if one fails, undue burdens will be placed upon the other members of the group. Strain and tension will be caused by the resulting frustration, and bitterness and division may bring the whole group to a standstill. While the organism may remain, its function is gone. Failure to accept responsibility may be seen at many points within the group. Some of the more serious areas of failure to accept responsibility are as follows:

Difficulty in Winning New Members. Most organizations find the objective of winning new members vitally important. The membership drives of the local PTA, YMCA or YWCA, and other community organizations are familiar. College fraternities and sororities though ostensibly selective compete frantically for certain pledges.

For the churches the winning of people is imperative, not merely important. The task of the church is evangelism. Indeed, there is serious question as to whether there is any other justification besides evangelism for a church's existence. By evangelism we should mean not only winning an individual but nurturing him into a fully matured Christian; this is the church's job.

Ordinarily the failure of a church group to win others is laid to lack of individual responsibility. Church members are very difficult to enlist in a consistent program of personal evangelism, and consequently the winning of new members to the church group is sharply curtailed. There are other reasons why more new members are not won. Sometimes outsiders are discouraged from joining churches because of the group's dissensions, its coldness or its theology. Others fail to be attracted to churches because membership is made too easy, and they see no challenge because no demands are made. Some people find it more challenging to become members of a lodge or fraternal organization rather than a church because more is expected of them.

Any failure of the church to win new converts and new members is an indication of illness. Barrenness may well lead to the church group's extinction. The story of our Lord's cursing of the barren fig tree (Matthew 21:19) seems always to leave many Christians conscience-stricken.

Difficulty in assimilating new members. Closely aligned to the problem of failure to win new members into a group is that of the failure to assimilate them once they have been won. The evangelistic efforts of many a church today remind one of someone trying to bail water out of a leaky rowboat with a wicker basket. The basket may start out full of water but soon loses most or all of it. C. E. Matthews, former Secretary of Evangelism for the Home Missions Board of the Southern Baptist Convention, admitted that failure in the conservation of the converts made in the Convention's evangelistic efforts was the most justifiable criticism that could be made against the work of the Convention. He figured that almost fifty percent of the current membership of Southern Baptist churches was lost to the cause of Christ.[14]

And few denominations have a better record. Most churches feel fortunate to get fifty percent of their total membership out to a morning service and are elated if fifty

---

[14]C. E. Matthews, *A Church Revival* (Nashville: The Broadman Press, 1955), pp. 102-103.

percent of the morning service attendants return for the evening service. What happens to the Sunday attendants at weekly services or meetings is even more discouraging. Most churchmen are painfully aware of this attendance problem and are honestly trying to remedy it. Whatever the causes of attendance failure and whatever the remedy, it is certain that the making of new members feel that they belong and are very much wanted stands high on the list of prescribed medicine.

Nonparticipation of members. Often the church group is rendered infirm not because it lacks the desire to integrate its constituency but because the constituents themselves simply do not cooperate. In such a case the group's task is four-fold — the preparation to integrate members, the challenge of inspiring members, the training to equip members, and finally action in using these members.

A church can prepare to integrate members into its activities by making a catalogue of the jobs which need to be done and by matching this job catalogue with the interests and talents of the new members. The challenge of inspiration should come strongly but not solely from the pulpit, for the Bible is rich in inspirational material to challenge new converts. Training new members in specific or technical tasks such as deaconship, Sunday school work, and youth work should be a continuous and well-planned part of the church program; recent developments in Christian Education have produced much help for church groups in this field. Once the new members have been prepared by challenge and training to participate, they must be utilized. One outstanding pastor was asked what he considered to be the major key to his success. His answer was that he used all his boards and committees; and his churches, pastored consecutively over a period of about thirty years, proved this for they were beehives of activity and life, making use of all members who would participate and sending dozens of young people into Christian service.

Now and then the stark reality of a hopeless situation arises. Every effort may have been made to inspire and elicit group cooperation and participation, and yet indifference, irresponsibility, lack of cooperation, and even open hostility prevail. In such a case dissolution of the group may be the wisest step. When a church group becomes set and is no longer productive, it ceases to have justification for existence. A stagnant, unproductive church might be wise to disband and reorganize under different conditions. This drastic action should not be taken until every effort at rehabilitation has been made. Instead of dissolving a sick group, why not do everything possible to restore its health? An earnest and consistent program for winning, assimilating, and utilizing as many members as possible will go far in accomplishing this objective. We must always remember the church in Jerusalem which had settled down in the early stages of stagnation until it was jolted by the persecutions which sent its members preaching the Gospel of Jesus Christ throughout the world.

Group Cohesion: Integrating or Disintegrating?

Disintegration is ordinarily not the exception in life, it is the rule. We are constantly fighting the deteriorative forces about us. This tendency of the universe to granulate or to run down is sometimes called entropy. Norbert Weiner describes the process as follows:

> As entropy increases, the universe, and all closed systems in the universe, tend naturally to deteriorate and lose their distinctiveness, to move from the least to the most probable state, from a state of organization and differentiation in which distinctions and forms exist, to a state of chaos and sameness. In Gibbs' universe order is least probable, chaos most probable. But while the universe as a whole, if indeed there is a whole universe, tends to run down, there are local enclaves whose direction seems opposed to that of the universe at large and in which

there is a limited and temporary tendency for organization to increase. Life finds its home in some of these enclaves.[15]

The universe including our material, social, intellectual, and ecclesiastical structure is constantly and relentlessly deteriorating. But there always have been and always shall be the islands of resistance or counteraction which are tirelessly stemming the tide of disintegration.

Forces making up this continual wave of disintegration are evils such as moral collapse, sensuality, greed, and indifference. Some of the opposing forces are law enforcement, educational institutions, the home, philanthropic interests, and supremely, the Church of Jesus Christ; these provide islands of positive resistance valiantly battling society's deterioration.

Within the churches as within all groups the deteriorating forces of entropy are constantly at work. The Christian must be aware of these forces in order to combat them. The following are especially harmful to group effectiveness.

Spiritual and social coldness, anxiety, excessive tensions, and dogmatism all have a debilitating effect upon group life. These are human attitudes, but they are also church-destroying attitudes. Paul confronted the Christians in Corinth with the peril of such attitudes as he excoriated them for their carnality and encouraged them to build upon the foundation of Christ Jesus.

Impulsiveness or precipitative action on the part of members have a disintegrating effect. Such conduct indicates immaturity of judgment and unwillingness to exercise careful, adequate evaluation of a total situation before making decisions. There is, of course, no virtue in delay, for little

---

[15]Norbert Weiner, *The Human Use of Human Beings* (second edition revised; Garden City, New York: Doubleday & Company, Inc., 1954), p. 12. (Originally published in Boston by Houghton Mifflin Company, 1950).

is gained by merely allowing time to pass. Confusion, fear, or even inaction may indicate stupidity, but impulsiveness and precipitative action may preclude solid and valuable consideration of significant problems. Precipitative action is often tempting, but maturity should help control it.

Lack of confidence in its leadership is another disintegrative force within a group. Whether this problem approaches the gigantic proportions seen in the repeated collapses of some foreign governments or the relatively minute incidents as encountered in church youth groups, it has catastrophic potentials for any organization.

The causes of such failure to have confidence in leaders may be legion, subtle, and elusive; they may be justified or not. But one important factor should stand out even though it may often be overlooked. The authority of a leader and of his communications to a group does not lie within himself but rather within the group's willingness to grant him authority. When that willingness or confidence deteriorates, so does the effectiveness of the leader and the group.[16] The understanding of this reality by pastors and other leaders should be an immense relief, not a humiliation. Authority is not an intrinsic and spontaneous attribute of a man's nature but a socially bestowed trust or gift upon one whose character (*ethos*) merits it. Roberto Michels writes:

> Whether authority is of personal or institutional origin it is created or maintained by public opinion, which in its turn is conditioned by sentiment, affection, reverence or fatalism. Even when authority rests on mere physical coercion it is accepted by those ruled, although the acceptance may be due to a fear of force.[17]

---

[16]See on this, Chester I. Barnard, *The Functions of the Executive* (Cambridge, Massachusetts: Harvard University Press, 1938), p. 163.

[17]Roberto Michels, "Authority," *Encyclopedia of the Social Sciences*, ed. Edwin R. A. Seligman and Alvin Johnson, (New York: Macmillan and Company, 1930), II, 319.

Trust and authority may also diminish. The group may lose confidence in its leadership for one reason or another. With loss of confidence integrative forces break down, and group cohesiveness is threatened. In such a situation the group may be faced with a sharp two-valued choice between new leadership or, if that is impossible, disbanding. Wise is the leader who steps aside when he senses that the group has withdrawn from him its trust of delegated authority.

High degrees of absenteeism, turnover or tardiness among members are a symptom of group disintegration. These are universal problems among groups. In 1955 the Research Committee of the Adult Education Association of the U.S.A. considered dropouts a major problem facing adult educators.[18] Industry has wrestled with the problems of absenteeism and tardiness and has cooperated in research seeking to understand and offset them.[19] The United States Armed Forces Institute recently reported high dropout rates and explored their causes.[20] Any research done tends to place the burden of responsibility upon the absentees rather than upon the organization. The study done by Bradt for USAFI[21] and the one he also did in collaboration with Carey[22] indicated that a great many adults of various groups dropped out for reasons which were personal and had nothing to do with the adequacy or inadequacy of the programs. Furthermore, the study of the USAFI dropouts indicated that approximately one-third of the participants in the program claimed that they had not enrolled for credit

---

[18]R. B. Spence and L. H. Evans, "Dropouts in Adult Education," *Adult Education*, VI (Summer, 1956), 221.

[19]Dorwin Cartwright and Alvin Zander, *op. cit.*, 319 ff.

[20]K. H. Bradt, *Why Service Personnel Fail to Complete USAFI Courses* (Washington: Department of Defense, Office of Armed Forces Information and Education, 1954).

[21]K. H. Bradt, *op. cit.*

[22]K. H. Bradt and J. T. Carey, *Why Students Drop Out* (Chicago: Center for the Study of Liberal Education for Adults, 1953).

and had quit the courses only after they had gotten out of them what they wanted.

Church members drop out of churches for reasons similar to those listed above. Personal problems as well as premature attainment of satisfaction each contribute to absenteeism. Churches and their personnel need to ask themselves whether they are adequately meeting needs. A strong program of evangelism which neglects conservation of members makes little sense. Any experienced pastor knows that initial converts come easier than revived absentees. Nevertheless, an attempt must be made to revive them, and programs for reclaiming inactive members can be found in much of the literature in the field of pastoral ministry and evangelism.[23] Reclamation efforts should be planned and executed in the church group to stem the tide of absenteeism, indifference and tardiness.

Group Communication: Effective or Deteriorating?

A final symptom of group health or illness has to do with the amount of decay present in the communication process of the group. In addition to the barriers to communication certain problems relating to the deterioration of group communication should be noted. Deterioration of communication may be caused by confusion and ambiguity in lines of communication within the group. Most groups are comprised of individuals who are arranged on some ladder of hierarchy of role and position. Most local churches put the pastor at the top of the hierarchy, followed by deacons,

---

[23]Consult such works as George Sweazey, *op. cit.*, Chap. XV; Andrew Blackwood, *Pastoral Leadership* (New York: Abingdon-Cokesbury Press, 1949), Chap. XVII; Roland Q. Leavell, *Evangelism Christ's Imperative Commission* (Nashville, Tennessee: Broadman Press, 1951), chap. XIV; C. E. Autrey, *Basic Evangelism* (Grand Rapids, Michigan: Zondervan Publishing House, 1959), Chap. 10; Sidney W. Powell, *Where Are the Converts?* (Nashville, Tennessee: Broadman Press, 1958); and others.

elders, or some other official board of leaders. These in turn are followed by other leaders, officers, and members. Each of these roles or positions is accompanied by its own peculiar authority and prestige. Ignorance or denigration of such roles or positions may lead to serious communication breakdown. Misunderstanding of communication lines or deliberate by-passing of normal channels may cause similar damage.

Deterioration of communication may be caused by over-evaluation or underevaluation of messages. Some messages are taken too seriously, and others are regarded too lightly. Our President is constantly confronted with the difficult task of balancing the value of messages about foreign affairs. For example, if he should underevaluate communist messages, he could encourage Red aggression through infiltration and perhaps even military coup. If he should overevaluate Communist messages, he could trigger vast military expansion in our own country courting economic disaster. Similarly a church's evaluation of messages must avoid extremes. Taking some messages too seriously could result in frustration, guilt and failure. Taking other messages too lightly could break the group's cooperation, confidence and morale.

Deterioration of communication also occurs if individual group members fail to speak when their communication is needed for adequate group functioning. A certain church was looking for a pastor. In the interim a young seminary graduate was preaching for the church Sunday after Sunday, and the members came to appreciate his work so much that they wanted him to take the job. Unfortunately, no one in the church spoke up for formally extending him a call. In the meantime he received an invitation from another church, and when he finally accepted it, the first church suffered from confusion and disappointment.

Our Lord found no one to speak in His behalf at the crucial moments of His trial and crucifixion. Paul berated the Corinthians for failing to speak against the fornicator they were allowing to remain in their fellowship. Indeed, among Paul's last words one reads an indictment against all those who fail to communicate when their testimony is needed most. The aged apostle cried: "At my first defense no one took my part; all deserted me. May it not be charged against them" (II Timothy 4:16 rsv). Many a promising missionary advance, many a progressive church proposal, and many a hopeful solution to a problem have died premature deaths because individuals within groups failed to speak when words of support would have saved them.

Serious deterioration in communication may prevail when contradictions occur between the formal and informal messages circulating within the group. Some time ago a church fellowship began to experience a communication breakdown. Formal and official policy was made public through various media; rumor and innuendo on the other hand circulated informally among the various members of the group. Informal messages charged that some group members were living contradictory to the formal policy of the group. Suspicion and intolerance exploded like fire in a parched forest, and the fellowship disintegrated.

Finally, deterioration of the lines of communication is seen when confusion and bewilderment characterize a group. Christ must have felt the pathos of this condition as He beheld the populace on His third tour of Galilee. Matthew tells us: "But when he saw the multitudes, he was moved with compassion on them, because they fainted, and were scattered abroad, as sheep having no shepherd" (Matthew 9:36). History has seen this condition repeated many times and probably no more vividly than now. As our Lord sees us, He must be moved with great compassion over us. Confusion and bewilderment reign over the broken church body of which He is ostensibly the head. Confusion and bewilderment cloud the churches' goals and functions. Some are preoccupied with fighting and dissension, others with serious service. Some are carrying out the great commission, while others are merely creating confusion. Some are seeking to integrate, others to disintegrate. Communication may be part of our vocabulary, but it is frequently foreign to our function.

The barriers or illnesses possible in communication might well cause one to despair of ever communicating within a group. But this would not be right. There are many healthy churches whose communication is effective. Their communication is multidirectional rather than one-way. Their formal and informal lines of communication are consistent. Their messages are authoritative, intelligent, and well received. Criticisms are voiced openly and forthrightly in appropriate ways. When the conditions of effective communication are fulfilled, group communication becomes healthy and so does a church.

III

The Renewal of the Church Group

Churches face problems all the way from spiritual apathy to group splitting, and therefore problem solving becomes a crucial point in church renewal. Perennial evangelism and persistent prayer may greatly profit the church, but sometimes they leave specific problems unsolved. These activities should be supplemented with other practical methods. Basically, there are two approaches to group problem solving.

Solving problems from the outside in. In group problem solving, this approach involves some form of authoritarianism. The pastor or other group leader conceives and develops policies himself. He proceeds under the delusion that he alone has the ability to invent ideas and administer procedures. Often underevaluating the talents of his group members, he in many instances fears members' intervention or participation as threats to his position. His orientation is dogmatic, and his mind closed; he frequently operates in terms of allness attitudes and the two-valued, either-or orientation.

Such an authoritarian or dictatorial approach tends toward a one-way communication procedure. The leader hands down his orders like a feudal lord. He allows no formal feedback, provides for no interpersonal exchange of ideas, and permits neither discussion nor debate of his ideas.

Such an approach obviously leads to group passivity. The members of the congregation become little more than puppets dancing at the ends of strings. With no share in policy making, they enjoy no interchange of ideas. They become part of the church's problem rather than its answer. Participation in this approach is limited solely to the carrying out of dictatorially imposed decrees. Such an approach to problem solving frequently leads to disinterest, dissatisfaction, and finally to open dissension.

Solving problems from the inside out. In sharp contrast to the solving of problems from the outside in, this approach seeks to involve as much of the church group as possible in problem solving and decision making. Rejecting any dictatorial philosophy, it adheres to democracy. In contrast to one-way communication procedures, this approach implies multi-directional communication, proceeding with the open minded, permissive attitude of togetherness. Verbal interchange among all members is encouraged. Both the verbal domination of a few on the one hand and the wallflower silence of some on the other hand are discouraged. In keeping with such a spirit, group passivity is bypassed in favor of group activity. All members are encouraged to help solve problems and make decisions. Under this method the members become part of the church's answer instead of its problem. This approach to group problem solving leads to group health.

Assuming that problem solving from the inside out is

better, two considerations are important. These have to do with the *methods* and *instruments* available to us for problem solving.

The Methods of Solving our Problems

Generally speaking, group problems fall into two areas, personality conflicts and conflict over policy methods.

Personality Conflicts

Full of explosive qualities, personality conflicts are individual in nature and yet group-wide in influence. Any given church group today is probably loaded with them. If the average minister standing up to preach on Sunday morning could pull back the cover of his people's lives and see revealed there the raw human needs, he would be appalled. Many realize this, but many don't. Bereavement, guilt, and many other personality problems make the average church a potential clinic for the maladjusted.

Cases involving personality maladjustments such as these are often serious and because of their very nature are usually kept within the circle of the individual's own private life. The pastor is ordinarily the only outsider who is consulted, and he should proceed to counsel the person accordingly. These personality problems usually do not erupt into social conflicts involving other members of the church group. If they should, however, the pastor and perhaps certain other members of the group may be forced to take action. What action should be taken?

The Christian church is provided with a general plan of action for such cases. It was set forth by our Lord who commanded:

> Moreover if thy brother shall trespass against thee, go and tell him his fault between thee and him alone: if he shall hear thee, thou hast gained thy brother. But if he will not hear thee, then take with thee one or two more, that in the mouth of two

or three witnesses every word may be established. And if he shall neglect to hear them, tell it unto the church: but if he neglect to hear the church, let him be unto thee as an heathen man and a publican (Matthew 18:15-17).

The steps of this plan are simple and practical providing for every factor in human relationships. Christ's plan contains the humanitarian elements of fairness both to the individual and to the group, of firmness, of reasonableness, and of responsibility. Above all, the plan is centered in forgiveness. The remainder of Matthew 18 deals with this crucial law. This factor of forgiveness remained in the mind of Peter during the whole discourse and finally goaded him to question the Lord concerning it. The text sets forth the classic conversation as follows:

Then came Peter to him and said, Lord, how oft shall my brother sin against me, and I forgive him? till seven times? Jesus saith unto him, I say not unto thee, Until seven times: but, Until seventy times seven (Matthew 18:21-22).

Even the parable of the unmerciful servant which followed was used by Jesus to illustrate forgiveness (Matthew 18:23-35).

Therefore this plan of forgiveness is the divinely inspired blueprint for church discipline, and to improve upon it would be impossible. It should be followed in dealing with the personality problems of individuals who are destroying the group. Because the plan is general, it can be supplemented with good counseling procedures.

Policy Problems

Matters of policy appear to be disassociated from personality problems, although in the strictest sense policy would be no problem except in people's minds. This aspect of problem solving will be approached without making a technical distinction. Most of the problems of policy or methods which arise in groups must be handled differently than those dealt with in the preceding section. How shall policy problems be settled?

Years ago, John Dewey put down a series of steps to be followed in solving problems which have become the expression of the highly successful scientific method. They are essentially as follows:

> A felt difficulty — the initial awareness of a problem;
> Location and definition of the problem;
> Suggested solution of the problem;
> Rational elaboration of the suggested solution;
> Observation and experiment leading to acceptance or rejection of the suggested solution.[24]

Dewey's method can be reduced or expanded to fit particular needs. In one form or another it has been widely used in scientific and social research. A variation of Dewey's method can facilitate problem solving for the church and groups within the church.

Develop the church's or smaller group's philosophy and goals so the group knows where it is going. The philosophy and goals of any church ought to be formulated by a competent committee and adopted by the group as a whole in formal action. Philosophy and goals should not be left to memory or tradition but should be accurately recorded in the group's constitution and bylaws. Each subgroup within the church such as the men's fellowship, the youth group, or a Sunday school class should understand that its philosophy and goals must be in keeping with those of the larger body and should not conflict with them. Once these factors are carefully established, the group will have a frame of reference in which to solve its subsequent problems. A word of caution ought to be advanced at this point. In the drawing up of the constitutional rules of the church or of one of its subgroups care should be taken to avoid

---

[24]John Dewey, *How We Think* (New York: D. C. Heath & Co., Publishers, 1910), p. 72.

the equally serious extremes of either laxity or rigidity. A constitution can be so vague and general as to be useless for the function of the group, and such laxity opens the way for group anarchy. On the other hand, a constitution can be so detailed, legalistic, and binding that it hamstrings the group in its function. A good constitutional committee can help the group avoid these extremes. Sample constitutions can be obtained from various denominational headquarters and from books in the field of pastoral work.

Define the church's major problems and put them on a priority list. The importance of this procedure is clear. No one can solve a problem until he knows what it is. Careful and precise definitions of the problems being considered may not merely simplify them but perhaps even eliminate them altogether. Many church problems when narrowed down and carefully defined suddenly appear to be a mere haggling over insignificant details.

There are various ways to define. The more common ways are by example, by class and differences, or by stipulation. Thus, definition of the term minister could appear as one of the following:

Definition by example: A minister is a man like the Rev. John Jones.

Definition by class and differences: A minister is a man ordained by a church to officiate at religious functions.

Definition by stipulation: The term minister means only those men ordained by the church as official clergymen.

For the average church problem, any one or more of these three methods of definition should suffice. The importance, however, of careful and painstaking work on defining the problem cannot be overstated, and the time spent on this one phase of problem solving may well mean time saved on the remainder of the project. So important is this factor of problem definition, space should be given to a list-

ing of the characteristics or rules of a good definition. J.
Jeffery Auer suggests the following:

> A good definition should be applicable to all situations or to
> all individuals included in the term defined.
> A good definition should exclude situations or individuals not
> included in the term defined.
> A good definition should not include the term being defined
> or any derivative of it.
> A good definition should be stated in terms that are simpler
> and more concrete than the term being defined.
> A good definition should not include connotative (implicative)
> terms.
> A good definition should be stated in terms that are suited to
> the particular audience.[25]

The group must decide whether the problems being considered should be placed on a priority list before or after
their careful definition. Advantages result from either choice.
But assigning priority before definition would seem prefer-
able, for this would insure the agreement of the group on
the comparative importance of each problem and therefore
which problem should be considered first. The main objective in adopting a priority list is to insure the highest
agreement possible in the group. Perfect agreement may
not be possible; therefore, majority rule should abide.

*Decide upon the several most reasonable solutions to
each problem.* This decision may be a relatively simple
process. Each offered solution within limits should be written on a blackboard where all the group can see it. Then by
a method of mutually agreed elimination strike out the
solutions which appear to be obviously inadequate. The result may be one or more solid possibilities for solution.
Individual comments and contributions should be encouraged and not stifled. Every reasonable solution should be
received and considered. With certain techniques for solic-
iting ideas wild notions are often advanced, and some of

---

[25]J. Jeffery Auer, *An Introduction to Research in Speech* (New
York: Harper & Brothers, Publishers, 1959), p. 70.

them have proved to be successful solutions to deep-seated problems. Timid members of a group will participate if encouraged and not cowed, and they are potentially fertile sources of ideas. They will clam up if embarrassed or carelessly brushed aside. When the suggested solutions have been narrowed to the most reasonable, the group is ready for the next step.

Subject each solution to a thorough critical evaluation. To a scientist working on a complex physical problem, this evaluation process may require many painstaking months or even years to complete. The amazing scientific advances in the world today attest to the advantages of patient labor. Our unwillingness to take such pains may well be the reason for much of our failure in the area of church problem solving.

Critical evaluation demands a relentless search for the facts supporting each solution. A fact is ordinarily thought of as something which can be known directly through sense experience. However, this definition would put facts strictly in the realm of physical objects, and the definition is inadequate. The bones that make up a man's cranium are facts, but so are the obsessions of that same man if he is insane. The definition of Larrabee, therefore, appears more adequate for our needs. He writes: "Whatever in experience is compelling, coercive, inescapable — whatever cannot be conjured into or out of our world at will — deserves the name of fact."[26]

This definition provides for mental activity as well as physical objects. In working with people, much of the importance of facts lies in the mental realm. In problem solving, therefore, first must come a relentless search for the facts of the situation. Rumor, exaggeration, oversimplification, distortion, and all other forms of misrepresentation

---

[26]Harold A. Larrabee, *Reliable Knowledge* (Boston: Houghton Mifflin Company, 1945), p. 128.

must be detected. The problem solver has to plunge to the heart of the matter, not being content merely with surface observation of a problem. Truth is often like an iceberg in that only a small portion of it is visible to the naked eye. Sometimes most of the truth is submerged beneath the surface, and the most relevant portion of it may not be seen.

Since the possible ways of distorting facts are legion, methods of digging out truth are often difficult and painstaking. Nevertheless, problem solving can be accomplished only when this part of our task is assiduously pursued. Objectivity and fact finding are indispensable tools for solving individual or group problems.

Decide upon the best solution. Proper critical evaluation should make the decision of the best solution relatively easy. If the group has thoroughly investigated the facts of a given problem, the strongest and most logical solution should be apparent. The group should then choose this alternative as the one most likely to solve the problem. Even then, the solution should be adopted tentatively and be accompanied by a willingness to change if necessary. Adoption of the chosen solution should be formal and democratic. Any major opposition to the solution should be viewed with genuine concern. No solution should be forced upon a majority of the group. Minor dissent may be expected because a solution may not always receive unanimous support.

Implement the solution through group participation. Such implementation may be carried out effectively through a committee or board, or a larger organization like the church school may work better. In some cases, the implementation should be put in charge of a single individual such as the pastor or the church school superintendent. If implementation suggests the entire church's participation, then the widest possible involvement should be sought. The nature of the problem as well as its most desirable outcome will determine which unit of people can implement the solution most successfully.

Check the results of the chosen solution and modify if necessary. A scientist does not assume that a given solution is necessarily the final one. A medical doctor tentatively prescribes a certain treatment for an illness; if it cures, he is satisfied. If it does not, he changes his first prescription and tries another until he discovers the correct one. Similarly in problem solving within a group a seemingly logical solution to a given problem may be tried; the leader and other group members should observe the solution to determine its effectiveness. If it does not solve the problem, then another solution should be tried, and so on until success is achieved. Group feedback is imperative in this process. If the feedback is analyzed, group problem solving can become effective and the group processes will be enhanced.

The Instruments for Solving Our Problems

Given an effective method for problem solving, the church group is left only with the task of implementing it. Traditional methods of implementation such as church business meetings have certainly proved their worth and should not be abandoned. These meetings can be made more effective through conscious use of modern group discussion methods and instruments centered around a basic plan of self-evaluation and corrective action which is vital to successful group life.

Self-Evaluation Through Group Discussion

Group self-evaluation may be enhanced through the use of some form of group discussion. Many of our churches need to take a good look at themselves. They must sit down and discuss their resources, personnel, and problems as well as their goals and philosophy. Several types of discussion could be used for this purpose.

Informal Group Discussion should probably be more frequently used. For its greatest effectiveness this type of discussion should be limited to small groups numbering not more than twenty. In such a group each member has a fair opportunity to participate and should be encouraged to do so.

A *panel discussion* could be utilized. The panel consists of a board of experts, of four to eight members, perhaps key leaders of the church, who talk over a problem in front of the rest of the group. Comments should be relatively short and unrehearsed. Interchange of ideas is encouraged, and after the problem has been adequately discussed by the panel, the chairman opens the meeting to audience participation. A variation of this method is that of having a speaker who is followed by a panel discussion. Sometimes a discussion meeting takes the form of an *open forum* in which the panel is dropped in favor of direct audience participation.

The symposium has been effective with many groups. A symposium usually involves a panel of experts who have prepared formal speeches on various phases of a given problem. Audience participation is encouraged through use of the question and answer period after the formal presentation.

If the time and qualified speakers are available, a *debate* may be planned. Debate involves two or more participants who compete in an effort to persuade others to accept or reject a given proposition as a basis for belief and action. Though highly persuasive in nature, debate is helpful because it allows rebuttal on the part of the opponents and thus requires all participants to defend their ideas. Other types of discussion may also require defense of ideas presented.

Now and then discussion bogs down. Time is wasted.

Members become tense and irritable or bored and disgusted, and the meeting may end in disappointment or stalemate. Churches have had business meetings that drifted into this problem; members begin to slip out of the meeting, and when time for the vote comes, there is no longer a quorum with which to do business officially. What can be done to avoid this?

Sometimes a *caucus* may prime the group's intellectual pump enough to settle a problem. The caucus simply endeavors to elicit the ideas and reactions of each member by asking each one of the group in turn to state his reactions. The advantages of this technique are obvious. Total participation, immediate review, clarification of ideas, and general consensus can be quickly provided.

Brainstorming has become a popular and productive method of breaking an impasse. In brainstorming all members contribute their ideas about possible solutions or courses of action. No criticisms, challenges, or even discussion of another's ideas are allowed. Even timid members are encouraged to participate, and their ideas are often valid. Even wildly implausible ideas are acceptable in a brainstorming session. Group workers have found that in some cases prejudices and assumptions have bound groups so tightly that the only answer to a problem may appear impossible. During the give and take process of brainstorming a problem, however, we see the situation in a new light. After all ideas have been contributed, they are turned over to a committee which sorts, utilizes, or eliminates them as it sees fit.[27]

The Buzz Session has been helpful when groups reach a stalemate. This device is actually a variation of brainstorm-

---

[27]For fuller discussion of brainstorming see Alex F. Osborn, *Creative Imagination* (New York: Scribners, 1957), and Charles H. Clark, *Brainstorming* (Garden City, New York: Doubleday & Company, 1958).

ing. The leader declares an intermission of a few minutes during which members in small groups of perhaps six talk about the point at issue. Chairs are dragged into small circles where members can closely face each other. Ideas are quickly thrown into the intimate conference. They are jotted down by a secretary and reported to the larger group when it is reconvened. After a short buzz session the larger group is often revitalized and again made ready to move.

Some workers have found an even smaller discussion unit helpful. It is called the *tête-a-tête* and is ordinarily used when a meeting is at a standstill because of differences between a few persons. When two or three individuals are seemingly stalemated over an issue or phrase of terminology, they are excused to another room. They can then discuss differences intimately until common ground has been established. When this has been done, they report back to the larger group.

A valuable method called a *resource input* has been used. This involves bringing in an outside resource expert to discuss the various aspects of a problem or the implications of a contemplated course of action. A lawyer might be asked to speak to a group about incorporating, or an architect might be asked to explain the process of renovation. The expert's remarks can be followed by an evaluation of the group's progress or question-and-answer period.

Stuart Chase advocated the Quaker practice of *silence* until agreement is reached.[28] Quakers refuse to make decisions or to take action until they have unanimous agreement. This may seem impossible, but Quakers get an amazing amount of work accomplished through this method, and studying it is profitable. Silence provides for a time of prayer and inward probing; it allows inner reflection upon

---

[28]Stuart Chase, *Roads to Agreement* (New York: Harper & Brothers, 1951), pp. 45-55.

the characteristics of the fellowship, and it gives us time to examine our consciences.

Sometimes *sociometry* helps a group evaluate itself. As originated by J. L. Moreno it was used to test the degree of groupness or integration of a group. With this tool members are asked to list on a piece of paper four or five other members of the group with whom they would most like to serve on a committee or associate with in some other way. The leader then draws a graph or a sociogram showing the direction and frequency of preferences within the group. Such a chart may reveal the nature of the group's integration or disintegration, the state of its group health or productivity, or the most compatible personnel to appoint for special committees. Sociometry can be a helpful tool in the right hands. In injudicious hands it can be injurious. A sociogram or graph should not be shown to the group as a whole. Some members would be hurt to see that they had not been frequently chosen or maybe not chosen at all. Others might be deeply disappointed that they had not been chosen by someone whom they most cherished. Then, if shown to the group as a whole, instead of becoming a tool to aid in group integration, the sociogram could accomplish the opposite. Discretion should be exercised in its use.

Sociodrama and *role playing* round out the list of techniques available for groups involved in problem solving. *Sociodrama* is a simplified form of dramatization used to clarify group problems in human terms. *Role playing* is an individual acting endeavor put on by a member of the group in the larger production called sociodrama. All of this is done extemporaneously without script or conscious effort for artistic effect.

All of us play roles in life. The role of husband, wife, minister, deacon, and many others are familiar to us. When one of these roles becomes inappropriate in our church group life, something must be done about it. Let us say, for example, that a deacon and a trustee cannot agree on the problem of the redecoration of the church. They may not be angry with each other, but they cannot agree. In role playing, one of the techniques is to have them argue their cases before the rest of the group. Then have them *reverse* their roles. Let each argue from his opponent's point of view. Each assumes the other's role and plays it to the hilt. Frequently when the roles have been reversed and played and the problem has been discussed by the group, differences disappear.

Sociodrama can be applied to many functions of group life. It is used to study human relations, to solve problems, to illustrate leadership, and to analyze group functioning. Sociodrama may use one or many individuals, and the great advantage lies in its spontaneity. The roles do not have to be thoroughly studied, action does not need to be carefully spelled out in a script, and no lines are memorized. Each person acts his selected role as he thinks it should appear. A role should be acted out as true to life as possible. In this way people and groups can see themselves reflected in the dramatization of the others. In the more refined areas of sociodrama various techniques are used such as self-expression technique, the collective-role presentation and the soliloquy technique.[29]

All these techniques of discussion and problem solving are usually helpful to groups which want seriously to evaluate their function and fellowship. As Shakespeare once put it, "The play's the thing wherein I'll catch the conscience of the king."[30]

---

[29]For a more complete discussion of these techniques see Elwood Murray, Raymond H. Barnard, and J. V. Garland, *Integrative Speech* (New York: The Dryden Press, 1953), and Alan F. Klein, *How to Use Role Playing Effectively* (New York: Association Press, 1959).
[30]William Shakespeare, *Hamlet*, Act II, Scene 2, Line 641.

Self-Evaluation Through Action Research

In recent years a new approach called Action Research has been utilized in studying groups. It approaches group study on the basis of the question, "How does this group work as-a-whole-in-action?" Instead of breaking the church group into small segments for study, this approach analyzes the group as a complete unit in action. It does not study such items as attitudes, membership rapport, and personnel as isolated entities, but it studies all of these factors as they operate together. The total group situation needs to be studied. We need to see the church-as-a-whole-in-action-in-its-environment. There are several ways in which this can be done. The church may bring in an action research director. This individual should know enough about groups and their problems to be able to spot weaknesses when they occur. The pastor of a church could do this job if he were to take the necessary time to do some reading in group dynamics and action research.

Another approach is to ask members of the group to fill out reaction sheets after a meeting is finished. These sheets should contain individual evaluations of the speaker, the presentation, the worth of what was said, the organization and production of the meeting, and even the physical environment mentioning heat, light, air, and other factors. The sheets are then correlated, tabulated, and the results given to the group at an appropriate time. Analysis of this feedback should reveal the strengths and weaknesses of the group's meetings.

Sometimes special observers are designated from the group to observe and evaluate its meetings. Afterward the observers report to the group on such factors as accomplishments of the meeting, multidirectional communication, individual participation, and points of agreement and disagreement.

These methods of self-evaluation for groups depend upon

seeing the group in operation as a total unit. No one person, problem, technique, or attitude should be assumed to be at fault, singled out, and then studied in isolation. Utilized as part of an evaluation program along with the previously discussed techniques of problem solving, these instruments of self-evaluation should aid the church group in the area of self-improvement. They may be of tangible value in helping to avoid tensions, misunderstandings, and controversies.

The church is made up of human beings. Because these human beings have been redeemed by the crucified and resurrected Christ does not mean they are perfect. And since the constituency is imperfect, the church is frequently plagued with problems. If one is apt to be critical of the church because of its problems, he must remember the purpose of the church is to provide a haven for those who need it. If the church appears to be overpopulated with the needy, perhaps it is succeeding. Nevertheless the church must have greater purity, unity, and effectiveness. To accomplish these goals every means of human endeavor and divine enablement should be grasped.

Centuries ago our Lord gathered around Him a little group. As individuals they were perverse, impetuous, and often strongly opinionated. As time went on, these followers learned the Christian meaning of fellowship. They worked, lived, and suffered together. Within a few short years their fellowship became warm, attractive, and desirable. Others watched them endure intense persecution and even martyrdom for their faith. This group became the church of Jesus Christ. The church has not always accomplished its goals nor fulfilled its assigned functions. But almost twenty centuries of existence have not tarnished its attractiveness. Men, women, and young people still seek its friendly environs. It may be bitterly attacked and viciously criticized by its enemies, but countless are the simple and direct testimonies of those who have sought it out and found it to be a haven. As Christians ours is the task of making the church a dynamic and desirable community which will continue to evoke within the hearts of men the deep desire expressed in that old Mennonite hymn:

> People of the living God, I have sought the world around;
> Paths of sin and sorrow trod, peace and comfort nowhere found:
> Now to you my spirit turns, turns a fugitive unblest;
> Brethren, where your altar burns, there receive me into rest.[31]

[31]*Church Hymnal* (Scottdale, Pa.: Mennonite Publishing House, 1951), p. 252.

Chapter Six

The Power to Communicate

KNOWLEDGE IS NOT ENOUGH. Familiarity with the tools of communication does not guarantee successful communication.

In addition to the tools, men need an inner power, a driving will, a spiritual dynamic making them *want* to communicate. Here Christianity makes its greatest contribution to communication. General semantics, cybernetics, field theory, group dynamics, and all other communication theories and methods may be likened to the sails of a ship; all of the equipment stands useless without the motivating winds of the Holy Spirit and New Testament Love. These two dynamic forces furnish the power for Christian communication.

I

THE POWER OF THE HOLY SPIRIT

Christianity has always held that the philosophy of humanism, which teaches that man is the center, or the measure of all things and that he is capable of self-direction, is not a sufficient approach to life. In his natural state a sinner who distorts the values of life, man turns airplanes into bombers, boats into battleships, and atomic energy into warheads. From Genesis to Revelation men rebel against God and one another.

Exceptions to humanistic rebellion are that whole host of Biblical and historical individuals who have shifted the center of their thinking from self to God. Theirs is not just the story of Judeo-Christianity but of Christian communication empowered by the Holy Spirit.

The Holy Spirit in Old Testament Communication

Although the Spirit of God evidently did not come upon all men in Old Testament times, He did enter those whom God selected from many walks of life to carry out His special will. God empowered many of these men so they could accomplish civil, military and spiritual feats; some of the Judges and Kings of Israel were surely inspired.

Others were empowered by God to proclaim His will and to record His word. All of the Old Testament shows the imprint of God's inspiration, but perhaps the prophetic writings most vividly depict this phase of his dealing with men.

The exact process of prophetic revelation and inspiration is not certain. The prophets themselves were convinced that their messages were the Word of God. Deuteronomy describes prophetic revelation and inspiration as an act wherein God put words in Moses' mouth and the prophet spoke to the people all that the Lord had commanded him (Deuteronomy 18:18). Some such process extended beyond Moses' time, for prophetic ministry was not confined to an isolated case or two in Israel's history. The long train of prophets from Moses' time to the close of the Old Testament is well known. Each successive prophet felt the burden of the Lord, and a variety of claims were written such as "Thus saith the Lord"; "The word of the Lord came unto me"; and "Hear the word of the Lord." How did these men receive their messages?

It seems that a combination of human and divine action took place. The variety of styles and emphases of the prophetic messages indicate that each prophet relayed to the recipients God-revealed and inspired messages in the prophet's own style. The true prophet was usually sensitive to God's presence and guidance. Even though the exact process is unknown, undoubtedly there were times when the prophet was deeply involved in prayer and meditation and was perhaps brooding over the condition of his people and the times. At such instances God would quicken his thought or even carry him away in a vision or trance-like state and reveal to him the message needed for the hour. John R. Sampey describes the phenomenon:

> We cannot understand fully the psychology of the prophets when inspired. Their mental processes were stimulated and guided by the Spirit, who clothed them with power. Imagination, memory, and reason were no doubt heightened, as well as intuition and spiritual insight. The Spirit of God chose proper men for His purpose, and then turned to account all their powers. The mind of the prophet perhaps varied from the extreme of trance and ecstacy all the way to a quiet thoughtfulness over which the Holy Spirit presided.[1]

Recording methods of the prophetic messages are also unknown. Nevertheless, these messages have been passed down in a form acceptable as canonical to the subsequent generations of Hebrews, approved by Christ (Matthew 5: 17-18), sanctioned by the apostles (Acts 2:16, cf. Acts 3: 24), and adopted by the church. These prophetic messages are among the greatest contributions to Christian communi-

---

[1]John R. Sampey, *Syllabus for Old Testament Study* (Nashville, Tennessee: Sunday School Board of the Southern Baptist Convention, 1924), p. 152.

cation, for they form part of the authoritative source material upon which Christian communication has constantly drawn.

The prophets contributed greatly to literary style. Andrew Blackwood writes: "Any student of world literature should agree that in literary form the writings of the prophets surpass the sermonic work of every other group."[2] Comparison of prophetic passages with the best in extra-Biblical sermonic literature reveals the amazing difference. The contrast here is great not because of any inferiority in modern preaching but because of the complete superiority of prophetic literature. Professor Blackwood further suggests:

> If such a lofty estimate seems extreme, try an experiment. For an hour or two read aloud from the most familiar chapters in the prophetic books, being sure to bring out the heartthrobs as they appear in the Hebrew rhythm. Then pick up a collection of more recent sermons, and do much the same with messages that you esteem most highly. If you know how to read, and how to bring out the music that lies hidden in words, you will feel that you have come down from the heights where the prophets dwell with God and that you move among the foothills from which you can view the alpine heights afar off. Good as you may find more than a few recent sermons, you cannot compare them with the prophetic oracles, which tower aloft like the Matterhorn, unmatched in all the world.[3]

Not only does such an experiment dramatize the superiority of prophetic literary style but also brings out the unique nature of Hebrew intuitive thought. It shows the difference between human genius and divine revelation.

The Holy Spirit in New Testament Communication

From the time of Christ to the Day of Pentecost the ministry of the Holy Spirit continued much as it did in

[2]Andrew Watterson Blackwood, *Preaching from Prophetic Books* (New York: Abingdon-Cokesbury Press, 1951), p. 18.
[3]*Ibid.*, p. 19.

Old Testament times. God's work was carried out only in a few individuals and for specific purposes. Thus the Holy Spirit came upon Mary in connection with the birth of Christ (Luke 1:35). He filled Elizabeth, mother of John the Baptist, and she pronounced a blessing upon Mary (Luke 1: 41 ff.). He visited Zacharias (Luke 1:67-79), Simeon (Luke 2:25-28), and John the Baptist (Luke 1:15 ff.). Even Jesus Christ carried out His ministry in the power of the Holy Spirit.[4]

Since the day of Pentecost the ministry of the Holy Spirit has been universal and constant among believers.[5] He empowered the apostles, early deacons, and others to such a degree that they went everywhere boldly communicating the Word of God (Acts 8:4). Thousands were converted and added to the church (Acts 2:41). Persecutors in Thessalonica paid bitter tribute to the converts' effectiveness by charging that, "These men who have turned the world upside down have come here also" (Acts 17:6 RSV). Working and preaching fearlessly in spite of persecution and martyrdom these early believers laid the foundation of the church and subsequent Christian communication. The Holy Spirit gave these men the inner power, the driving will, and the spiritual dynamic to communicate effectively.

The history of Christianity continues this story. God spoke powerfully through such men as Augustine, Martin Luther, John Wesley, and D. L. Moody. These men full of divine spiritual power reformed the church and evangelized the masses.

Many still feel that the Gospel can be communicated powerfully with the help of the Holy Spirit. In 1950 the

----

[4]See such passages as Matthew 3:16-17 and parallels; also Luke 4:18-19; and Acts 10:37-38.

[5]See such passages as John 14:16-17; I Corinthians 3:16; 6:19; Romans 8:9.

author conducted a survey investigating the place of the Holy Spirit in preaching.[6] Questionnaires were sent to 102 leading evangelical ministers in the United States and Canada. Sixty-two returned the questionnaires. The study revealed a continuing conviction among evangelicals that Spirit-filled preaching is both possible and necessary. Most of the contributors felt that present-day preachers can have the power of the Holy Spirit as did the apostles and prophets of old. Inspiration for continued recording of scripture was, of course, ruled out. A large majority of respondents felt that they knew when they were preaching in the power of the Holy Spirit; others expressed some uncertainty about this. The major reasons for feeling the Spirit's power in preaching were liberty of sermon delivery, an inexplicable outside motivation, and results from the sermons. Most of those who returned the questionnaire thought that a significant difference exists between preaching in the power of the Holy Spirit and preaching that results from thorough preparation, personal magnetism, good psychology, and rhetorical persuasion. Others felt that the Holy Spirit uses such means.

When asked what difference might exist between the two types of preaching, those who claimed a difference mentioned such things as results, lack of artificiality, and the feeling of spiritual power. Some practical results of preaching in the power of the Holy Spirit were mentioned such as conviction of sin, conversion, progress of evangelism and missions, manifestation of the fruits of the spirit, and unity and high morale in the church. Such responses from leaders of the evangelical church cannot easily be ignored. Most of the respondents to the questionnaire have enjoyed conspicuously effective ministries. In every case

---

[6]Raymond W. McLaughlin, "The Place of the Holy Spirit in Preaching" (unpublished Doctor's dissertation, Northern Baptist Theological Seminary, Chicago, 1950).

they insist that their communicative powers come from divine as well as human sources. Most of them are well trained, diligent men; however, each recognizes the necessity and the possibility of communicating with spiritual power. When asked to list the prerequisites of preaching in the power of the Holy Spirit, they suggested such practices as prevailing prayer, surrender and obedience to God, cleanliness of life, belief in the authority and power of God's Word, thorough preparation, and faith in the Spirit's power.

Not all Christians communicate with spiritual power. The barrier seems to be individual self-centeredness. Sometimes people talk, counsel, or preach with a selfish motive. Desire for personal display, social prestige and other questionable motives are not in keeping with Christianity and cannot help but rob the Christian of effectiveness. When an individual turns from a self-centered life to a Christ-centered life, spiritual power comes. Once this inner dynamic motivates an individual, he will want to communicate. Equipped with a broad understanding of communication techniques and filled with the power of the Holy Spirit, the Christian is willing and able to communicate to the world with tenderness and love.

II

THE COMMUNICATIVE POWER OF LOVE

The outward expression of Christian communication must be love. New Testament love is both verbally and non-verbally communicated. It is the outward expression of the inner spiritual power which makes an individual want to communicate.

Paul's treatise on love in the thirteenth chapter of First Corinthians succinctly presents the heart of the Christian communication process. It is the most penetrating challenge to a life of love found in all of literature. The dynamics necessary for most efficient communication accompany true love. Without love, one may have mastered communication methodology and yet not communicate. Because there is so much vagueness and confusion if not complete misunderstanding about the term love as it is being used here, a word of explanation is due.

Basically, two types of love have been operative in man. They can be traced back to ancient civilizations although they are still referred to by their Greek terms, eros and agape.[7] Despite a certain amount of overlapping with agape, eros-love, a theory prevalent in the ancient Hellenistic world, depended for its existence upon the value of the beloved; the more desirable the object, the more passionate the eros-love.

Eros-love, in the hands of some modern writers, has been linked strongly with sensual love. While one cannot separate the existence of this quality from eros, to make sex or sensuality the dominant quality of this type of love is to do it injustice. The Platonic concept of eros was such as to constantly challenge a person to overcome sensual impulses. Nevertheless, even in its highest form eros was essentially egocentric, and as such it is found in all humanity. Indeed, while it is true that eros is never mentioned in the New Testament by name, the drift of some contemporary believers in Christianity is toward an eros-love for God that is essentially selfish and egocentric far more than it is toward agape or unmotivated love.

In sharp contrast to the eros of the Hellenistic world, primitive Christianity conceived of love as agape. Agape-love was not motivated by some object outside the individual; in fact, agape was indifferent to external values. Agape-love is the type of love demanded by Jesus when

[7]See Anders Nygren, *Agape and Eros*, trans. Philip S. Watson (S.P.C.K., 1953).

He said, "But I say unto you, love your enemies, bless them that curse you, do good to them that hate you, and pray for them which despitefully use you, and persecute you . . ." (Matthew 5:44). Jesus emphasized this type of love to challenge His disciples to a kind of life which would differ significantly from those living in paganism. He explained His command by saying:

> For if ye love them which love you, what reward have ye? do not even the publicans the same? And if ye salute your brethren only, what do ye more than others? do not even the publicans so? Be ye therefore perfect, even as your Father which is in heaven is perfect (Matthew 5:46-48).

Agape causes us to love the unlovely and the unattractive. Agape gives us compassion for the repulsed and the rejected. Agape inspires concern for the uncouth, the ungraceful, and the handicapped. Agape leads us to return love for loathing and compassion for condemnation.

Paul proposes in I Corinthians 13 that agape-love is the most vital factor in life. Such a life of love is mandatory to effective communication of the Gospel of Christ to others. An analysis of I Corinthians 13 indicates that there are at least three basic reasons why this is true.

The Tragedy of Love's Absence

Men are notoriously susceptible to self-deceit. It is hard not to rate ourselves better than we really are. The apostle Paul described this pathetic malady of self-deceit in his epistle to the Galatians: "For if a man think himself to be something, when he is nothing, he deceiveth himself" (Galatians 6:3). In the first three verses of I Corinthians 13 Paul concretely illustrates this disease. He charges, in effect, that the tragedy of love's absence is best seen in the man who is something, yet nothing.

One may be eloquent as an orator but, without love, as empty as clouds without water. Our ververbalized generation falls easy prey to this hazard. To talk is so simple, and yet it is so difficult to live and love. Research indicates that the average American spends about seventy percent of his active hours communicating on the verbal level. This is spent listening, speaking, reading, and writing in that order.[8] On this basis each of us spends approximately 10 or 11 hours every day participating in verbal communication. If during this time the nonverbal communication of our love reinforces the verbal communication of our mouths, then we will not be failures. Unfortunately, Christians tend to become too preoccupied with the words and forget the love. Many a well-meaning believer seems to think that mental and verbal assent to orthodox doctrines assures him of eternal salvation. Belief is, of course, mandatory for salvation, but agape-motivated action is mandatory for the communication of salvation. We must not forget the Biblical injunction, "But be ye doers of the word, and not hearers only, deceiving your own selves" (James 1:22). Success as a Christian, more than in any other area of life, depends upon the demonstration of agape, not just orthodox phrases.

One of the greatest temptations before the Christian preacher is that of pulpit oratory divorced from pastoral love. Few ministerial activities can parallel the thrill to the preacher of standing before a great audience and holding it spellbound by a well-prepared and effectively delivered sermon. As a matter of fact, few professions offer as much opportunity for such expression as does the Christian ministry; but therein lies the snare of the devil. To a preacher with such temptations the words of Paul are appropriate, "Though I speak with the tongues of men and of angels, and have not love, I am become as sounding brass, or a tinkling cymbal" (I Corinthians 13:1).

---

[8]Paul T. Rankin, "The Importance of Listening Ability," *English Journal,* College Edition XVII (October, 1928), 623-30.

Furthermore Paul says, a man though promising, may be a disappointment as a prophet. He may have super-human insight into the future, superior understanding of situations which to most men are complete mysteries, and knowledge which is vast and penetrating, and yet be a tragic failure because he does not balance these gifts with agape-love. Most theologians feel that these superhuman gifts mentioned by Paul are seldom, if ever, seen in our contemporary society. But this only intensifies the thrust of Paul's knowledge, for without agape-love, these gifts would be useless.

Again, Paul suggests that a man may succeed and yet fail as a pietist, ". . . and though I have all faith, so that I could remove mountains, and have not love, I 'am nothing" (I Corinthians 13:2). Many Christians today have dedi-cated themselves to the keeping of the faith. Being set for the defense of the Gospel is a noble, necessary, and impor-tant task. But when a man defends the Gospel without love, he is nothing. Winston Churchill upon beholding a pompous pietist pass one day is reported to have com-mented, "There, but for the grace of God, goes God."

Some believers in our day create the same impression. They reek with saccharine-like piety, but they appear to be devoid of love. While succeeding at one task, they have failed in the long run.

Moreover, the passage indicates that a man may be something yet nothing as a philanthropist. One may build libraries and hospitals all over the world and yet with-out love be nothing. One may finance the construction of magnificent religious cathedrals and influential social institutions and yet, without love, be a spiritual void.

Paul also warns us that a man may be something yet nothing as a martyr. ". . . and though I give my body to be burned, and have not love, it profiteth me nothing" (I Corinthians 13:3). In the early days of Christian history, martyrdom evidently became popular, and some sought it.

But the lives of Christ and His followers during New Testament times never show deliberate plans for death among them. Quite the contrary was true. Christ and the apostles studiously avoided death though they were willing to endure it if there was no alternative. Martyrdom for martyrdom's sake would surely be self-centered and therefore devoid of agape-love. Any man calculating such a death would be, in Paul's thinking, a colossal failure.

Lovelessness penetrates the church in varying degrees. Some churches are afflicted with it more than others. Few are immune to it. In the struggle for orthodoxy Christians have developed a cluster of little middle-class groups into which the initiated are readily welcomed but the aliens are shunned. We have our own unwritten protocol, caste systems, theological pigeonholes, and carefully defined jargon. Facility in the use of our own private vernacular is mandatory. All in all we Christians have spun about ourselves tight little cocoons insulating us from the tragic needs of a confused society. We need seriously to contemplate the penetrating analogy of Theodore Wedel who described our plight as follows:

> Picture a coastguard or life-saving station on a dangerous coast. It has stood for centuries, and tales of its rescue service are treasured by the successors of the founders. In the course of time, indeed, those who manned the rescue service turned to expanding and beautifying the station itself. Do not "lifesavers" deserve comfort and a rest home to fit them for their arduous task? Architects vied with one another in building for them a dwelling place worthy of their vocation. Honorary though not active members joined in lending support. Nor was the rescue station designed merely for those whose duty it was to launch the lifeboats. The rescued in their turn deserved warm beds and proper food.
>
> The station-building, however, became in time such an absorbing activity that rescue service itself was increasingly neglected, although traditional rescue drills and rituals were carefully preserved. The actual launching out into ocean storms became a hireling vocation or one left to a few volunteers. What was even more a deflection of the original charter of the

station, when the dedicated volunteers brought in their boat loads of the shipwrecked — men of alien color and speech, maimed and encrusted with ocean slime — the custodians of the rescue station were disconcerted and disturbed. "Will they not," so they were tempted to exclaim, "soil the linen on our clean beds, and, moved by gratitude for salvation, desire to become lifesavers themselves and thus presume to belong by right to our intimate fellowship? Should we not set up a minimum entrance requirement of cleanliness and good manners before we offer shelter? We can, at least, urge them to build a life-saving station of their own at a decorous distance from our own.[9]

Though this analogy could almost indefinitely be extended, it portrays our decadent state. We must wake up before it is too late. We must not be part of the tragedy caused by the absence of love.

The Blessing of Love's Presence

The second reason making agape-love the most vital factor in life is the unspeakable blessing brought by the presence of this love (I Corinthians 13:4-7). What does this mean in definite terms? Paul approaches this aspect of the subject by discussing love's negative and positive factors.

Negatively, he describes what Thomas Chalmers once called, "The expulsive power of a new affection."[10] Thus, agape-love rejects such negative factors in life as egocentricity, jealousy, arrogance, resentment, and rejoicing in another's failures. These unwholesome traits of personality frequently underlie communication breakdowns, for they are the antithesis of Christian love and the epitome of human self-centeredness. This gnawing malady of egocentricity can only be overcome by the expulsive power of

---

[9]Theodore O. Wedel, "Evangelism at Evanston," reprinted from *Christianity and Crisis*, XIV (April 19, 1954).

[10]Thomas Chalmers, "The Expulsive Power of a New Affection," *The Protestant Pulpit*, comp., Andrew Blackwood (New York: Abingdon-Cokesbury Press, 1947), p. 50.

agape-love. Unfortunately, the modern view of life, far from envisioning what can be contributed to others, preoccupies itself with the greedy motive of, "What's in it for me?"

Paul not only condemned the negative factors which are hostile to agape, but he proceeded to expound the expressive power of a positive possession. Agape-love, he suggested, is patient, kind, overjoyed with right-doing, all-bearing, all-believing, all-hoping, all-enduring, and all-suffering. Compare these positive personality traits with the negative, and observe the radical differences. Characteristic of the selfless individual, the positive factors are seen in healthy interpersonal communication, and they are the essence of the man dominated by agape-love.

Few blessings are as desperately needed today as this kind of agape-love. A constant clamor of voices arises offering panaceas for the world's ills. Education, world government, science, and other disciplines are offered as the answer to humanity's evils. Any of these would work if motivated by and pervaded with agape. Without love, all will fail. Conversely, we could survive without education if we had love. We could get along without world government if we had love. We could even progress without science if we had love. But we cannot survive with any discipline devoid of New Testament love. It is man's "indispensable emotion,"[11] the unspeakable blessing of love.

The Glory of Love's Endurance

Finally, the Apostle climaxes his argument by describing for us the glory of love's endurance (I Corinthians 13: 8-13). To dramatize this notion he presents two profound and contrasting laws of life.

----

[11]Harry and Bonaro Overstreet, *The Mind Alive* (New York: W. W. Norton & Company, 1954), p. 50.

First, Paul recognizes the law of the temporal. Some things in life are transient. The activities he cites which eventually will pass away are treasured experiences cherished by many. Accordingly regardless of how much importance we may attach to prophecy, whether forthtelling or foretelling, it shall pass away. In like manner, speaking in tongues, a controversial subject for contemporary Christianity, shall some day cease. Even knowledge, venerated by every generation and the supposed panacea for the world's ills in the minds of many, also shall pass away.

Heraclitus, an ancient Greek philosopher, once contended that a man could never step into the same river twice. He meant that because of the changing character of both the river and the man, such an action would be impossible. Interpersonal communication must take such reality into account. Our evaluations of the life about us must recognize the everchanging panorama of our universe and adapt to it. Our language, made up of verbal symbols that tend to be static, must be used in such a way as to reflect this constant process of change. Agape-love will give us the spiritual strength to make such adjustment possible.

Paul then turns from the law of the temporal to the law of the eternal. If it is distressingly true that some of our prized possessions in life shall pass away, it is also reassuringly true that the more crucial factors of life shall endure. We could conceivably get along without prophecy, speaking in tongues, and knowledge. But mankind cannot exist without faith, hope, and love. These latter three Paul assures us will abide. He treats them comparatively to dramatize the superiority of the last.

Faith therefore is listed as one of the great and abiding truths of life. Faith in God, Christ, the Bible, and one another makes any continued existence possible. Men ". . . contend for the faith once delivered unto the saints" (Jude 3). They preach it, live it, defend it, and sometimes die for it. William Ellery Channing said, "Faith is love taking the form of aspiration."[12] Thomas S. Jones in one of his *Quatrains* pointed to the comfort of faith, writing:

> Faith is the cliff on which the weak wave breaks,
> The tree around whose might frail tendrils twine,
> In cloudy skies it sets a starry sign,
> And in the sorrowing soul an altar makes.[13]

There are those to whom faith, whether temporal or eternal, means little. Their view has been expressed eloquently by A. C. Swinburne who wrote: "Faith, haggard as Fear that had borne her, and dark as the sire that begat her, Despair."[14] But to most of us Christ has made faith vital, and we would prefer to sing with Tennyson:

> Strong Son of God, immortal love,
> Whom we, that have not seen thy face,
> By faith, and faith alone, embrace,
> Believing where we cannot prove.[15]

Hope is also listed by Paul as one of the great and abiding truths of life. Mankind lives, works, suffers, and even dies for hope. Emil Brunner voiced the significance of hope to human life when he said:

> What oxygen is for the lungs, such is hope for the meaning of human life. Take oxygen away and death occurs through suffocation, take hope away and humanity is constricted through lack of breath; despair supervenes, spelling the paralysis of intellectual and spiritual powers by a feeling of the senselessness and purposelessness of existence. As the fate of the human

---

[12]William Ellery Channing, *Note-Books: Faith.*

[13]Thomas S. Jones, *Quatrains.*

[14]A. C. Swinburne, "An Autumn Vision," VII, 1, 9. Taken from Sir Edmund Gosse, and Thomas Wise (eds.), *The Complete Works Of Algernon Charles Swinburne* (London: William Heinemann Ltd., Publishers and New York: Gabriel Wells, Publishers, 1925).

[15]Alfred Lord Tennyson, "In Memoriam," Introduction. Taken from *The Poetic And Dramatic Works of Alfred Lord Tennyson* Cambridge Edition (Boston and New York: Houghton Mifflin Company, 1898), p. 163.

organism is dependent on the supply of oxygen, so the fate of humanity is dependent on its supply of hope.[16]

To the whole world the Christian testifies of his hope in Christ as God's means of eventual intervention in the hopeless affairs of men. In the words of Paul we are,

> Looking for that blessed hope, and the glorious appearing of the great God and our Saviour Jesus Christ; Who gave himself for us, that he might redeem us from all iniquity, and purify unto himself a peculiar people, zealous of good works (Titus 2:13-14).

Thus faith is a magnificent quality to demonstrate to an unbelieving world. It is imperative, and without it we perish. Hope is a valiant reason for living to hold aloft before the jaded senses of a despairing humanity. Without hope we lose our incentive, our purpose for existing.

But towering far and above both of these superior attributes, as the mountains tower above the plains, is the superlative life of agape-love. Love is listed by Paul as the last great and abiding truth. ". . . The greatest of these is love" (I Corinthians 13:13). Mankind has taken a long time to become aware of this but we are learning. Men are beginning to learn that the energy of love is as real as physical and mind energy. For human survival it is more vital than either.

The contemporary world had heard little of Dr. Paul Carlson until late in 1964. Then it was suddenly made aware of him during a crisis in the Congo. Carlson was a Christian doctor, a medical missionary sacrificially serving African nationals. Rather than leave his patients during the dangerous rebellion, Dr. Carlson stayed at his hospital in Wasolo after evacuating his family. He was captured by

---

[16]From *Eternal Hope,* by Emil Brunner, trans. by Harold Knight. (Published in the U.S.A. by the Westminster Press, 1954), p. 7. Used by permission.

rebel forces, taken hostage, and along with a group of other prisoners shot to death before he could escape. The free world honored this Christian martyr. They saw in him factors which our culture considers important — education, scientific orientation, and religious faith. But the one thing that stood out above all these factors was his sacrificial love for unfortunate people. Separating himself from the vast majority of educated, scientifically trained, and religious people of this generation, he had turned his back upon the luxuries of our culture and given himself in agape-love to those who could scarcely repay that devotion. This is the kind of energy needed to heal society.

III

SHALL WE COMMUNICATE?

At the close of Chapter One we claimed that Christians can improve their communication. The tools for this improvement stand ready. Knowledge of the communication process and the will to communicate are the prerequisites.

The process of communication has been set forth in the major portion of this book. The Christian who wishes to do so may learn and understand that process. Nothing short of complete mastery of one's tools is acceptable for effective communication. Given adequate tools and a driving will, the Christian can share the truth with others.

The power to communicate is also available. Not long before Christ was crucified, He promised His followers:

> And I will pray the Father, and he will give you another counselor, to be with you forever, even the Spirit of truth, whom the world cannot receive, because it neither sees him nor knows him; you know him, for he dwells with you, and will be in you (John 14:16-17 RSV).

And just before His ascension He reminded them, "And behold, I send the promise of my Father upon you; but stay in the city, until you are clothed with power from on high" (Luke 24:49 RSV).

Pentecost and subsequent events recorded in the Book of the Acts as well as post-apostolic church history attest to the effectiveness of this power to communicate. Accessible today, this power can issue forth from Christian lives in an irresistible demonstration of agape-love. Without the power of the Holy Spirit and the resulting demonstration of selfless love, Christians lack not only the ability to communicate but also any serious reason for existence.

Early in His ministry our Lord gathered His followers together on a hillside. There He gave them a message which has subsequently been called His "Sermon on the Mount." Among other piercing challenges in that message, He asked,

> For if ye love those who love you, what reward have you? Do not even the tax collectors do the same? And if you salute only your brethren, what more are you doing than others? Do not even the Gentiles do the same? You, therefore, must be perfect, as your heavenly Father is perfect (Matthew 5:46-48 RSV).

Few questions penetrate more deeply into the heart of Christian sharing. Do we love more? Do we communicate better? Do we live more selfless lives than those who are not Christians? Christian love, Christian character, Christian communication — these three — they are the stuff of Christian sharing. In the words of our Lord,

What do ye more than others?

Bibliography

Ayer, A. J., *et. al. Studies in Communication.* London: Martin Secker and Warburg Ltd., 1955.

Bachman, John W. *The Church in the World of Radio-Television.* New York: Association Press, 1960.

Baird, A. Craig. *Argumentation, Discussion, and Debate.* New York: McGraw-Hill Book Company, Inc., 1959.

Barnard, Chester I. *The Functions of the Executive.* Cambridge, Massachusetts: Harvard University Press, 1938.

Baugh, Hansell. *General Semantics.* New York: Arrow Editions, 1938.

Bennett II, Thomas R. *The Leader and the Process of Change.* New York: Association Press, 1962.

Berlo, David. *The Process of Communication.* New York: Holt, Rinehart and Winston, 1960.

Blackwood, Andrew. *Pastoral Leadership.* New York: Abingdon-Cokesbury Press, 1949.

Bois, J. Samuel. *Explorations in Awareness.* New York: Harper & Brothers, 1957.

————————. *The Art of Awareness: A Textbook on*

213

General Semantics. Dubuque, Iowa: Wm. C. Brown Company Publishers, 1966.

Boyd, Malcolm. *Christ and Celebrity Gods the Church in Mass Culture.* Greenwich, Connecticut: The Seabury Press, 1958.

————. *Crisis in Communication.* Garden City, New York: Doubleday & Company, Inc., 1957.

Briggs, Harold E. *Language . . . Man . . . Society Readings in Communication.* New York: Rinehart & Company, Inc. Publishers, 1949.

Brown, Roger. *Words and Things.* Glencoe, Illinois: The Free Press, 1958.

Buchanan, Paul C. *The Leader and Individual Motivation.* New York: Association Press, 1962.

Butler, H. E. (trans.). *The Institutio Oratoria of Quintilian.* 4 Vols. Cambridge, Massachusetts: Harvard University Press, 1953.

Carnell, Edward J. *The Kingdom of Love and the Pride of Life.* Grand Rapids, Michigan: Eerdmans Publishing Company, 1960.

Cartwright, Dorwin, and Alvin Zander, (eds.). *Group Dynamics Research and Theory.* second edition. New York: Row, Peterson and Company, 1960.

Casteel, John L. (ed.). *Spiritual Renewal Through Personal Groups.* New York: Association Press, 1957.

Chase, Stuart. *Guides to Straight Thinking with 13 Common Fallacies.* New York: Harper & Brothers, 1956.

————. *The Proper Study of Mankind.* New York: Harper & Brothers, 1948.

————. *The Tyranny of Words.* New York: Harcourt Brace and Company, 1938.

————, and Marion Tyler Chase. *Power of Words.* New York: Harcourt Brace and Company, 1954.

————, and Marion Tyler Chase. *Roads to Agreement.* New York: Harper & Brothers, 1951.

Cherry, Colin. *On Human Communication.* Cambridge: Technology Press of Massachusetts Institute of Technology, 1957.

Chisholm, Francis P. *Introductory Lectures on General Semantics.* Lakeville, Connecticut: Institute of General Semantics, 1945.

Clark, Charles H. *Brainstorming.* Garden City, New York: Doubleday & Company, 1958.

Cooper, Lane (trans.). *The Rhetoric of Aristotle.* New York: D. Appleton Century and Company, 1932.

DeWire, Harry A. *The Christian as Communicator.* Philadelphia: The Westminster Press, 1961.

Dillistone, F. W. *Christianity and Communication.* London: Collins, 1956.

Dubois, Rachel Davis, and Mew-Soong Li. *The Art of Group Conversation.* New York: Association Press, 1963.

Eisenson, Jon. *The Psychology of Speech.* New York: F. S. Crofts & Company, 1938.

Elliot, Grace Loucks (ed.). *How to Help Groups Make Decisions.* New York: Association Press, 1959.

Etc.: A Review of General Semantics. Official Organ of the International Society for General Semantics. Editorial Office: San Francisco State College, San Francisco 94132.

Ferre, Frederick. *Language, Logic and God.* New York: Harper & Row, Publishers, 1961.

Fromm, Eric. *The Art of Loving.* New York: Harper & Brothers, 1956.

The General Semantics Bulletin. Official Organ of the Institute of General Semantics. Rural Delivery, Lakeville, Connecticut, U.S.A.

Gorman, Mother Mary. *The Educational Implications of the Theory of Meaning and Symbolism of General Semantics.*

Washington, D.C., The Catholic University of America Press, 1958.

Guetzkow, Harold. *Groups, Leadership and Men.* Pittsburgh: Carnegie Press, 1951.

Hall, D. M. *Dynamics of Group Action.* Danville, Illinois: Interstate Printers and Publishers, Inc., 1957.

Hall, Edward T. *The Silent Language.* Greenwich, Connecticut: Fawcett Publications, Inc., (Premier Books), 1959.

Hare, A. Paul, Edgar F. Borgatta, and Robert F. Bales. *Small Groups Studies in Social Interaction.* New York: Alfred A. Knopf, 1955.

Hayakawa, S. I. in consultation with Basil H. Pillard, *Language in Thought and Action.* New York: Harcourt Brace & Company, 1949.

————————————, (ed.). *Language, Meaning and Maturity.* New York: Harper & Brothers, 1953.

Henry, Carl F. H. *Christian Personal Ethics.* Grand Rapids, Michigan: Wm. B. Eerdmans Publishing Company, 1957.

Hoch, Paul H., and Joseph Zubin (eds.). *Psychopathology of Communication.* New York and London: Grune & Stratton, 1958.

The Holy Bible. In various versions.

Homans, George C. *The Human Group.* New York: Harcourt, Brace and Company, 1950.

Howe, Reuel L. *The Miracle of Dialogue.* New York: Seabury Press, 1963.

Huff, Darrell. *How to Lie with Statistics.* New York: W. W. Norton & Company, 1954.

Jeans, Sir J. H. *Eos, or the Wider Aspects of Cosmogony.* London: Kegan, Paul, Trench, Trubner, and Company, Ltd., 1928.

Jennings, Helen H. *Leadership and Isolation.* Second edition. New York: Longmans, Greene & Co., Inc., 1950.

Johnson, Wendell. *People in Quandaries the Semantics of Personal Adjustment*. New York: Harper & Brothers, 1946.

The Journal of Communication. A publication of the National Society for the Study of Communication. R. Wayne Pace, Executive Secretary, Department of Speech, University of Montana, Missoula, Montana, 59801.

Kendig, M. (ed.). *Papers from the Second American Congress on General Semantics: Non-Aristotelian Methodology (applied) for Sanity in Our Time*. Chicago: Institute of General Semantics, 1941.

Kierkegaard, Soren. *Works of Love*. Trans. Howard and Edna Hong. New York: Harper & Brothers, 1962.

Klein, Alan F. *How to Use Role Playing Effectively*. New York: Association Press, 1959.

Knowles, Malcolm Shepherd, and Hulda Knowles. *Introduction to Group Dynamics*. New York: Association Press, 1959.

Korzybski, Alfred. "An Outline of General Semantics: the Applications of Some Methods of Exact Sciences to the Solution of Human Problems and Educational Training for General Sanity." *Papers from the First American Congress on General Semantics*. Chicago: The Institute of General Semantics, 1938.

_____. *Manhood of Humanity*. Second edition. Lakeville, Connecticut: The International Non-Aristotelian Library Publishing Company, 1950.

_____. *Science and Sanity: An Introduction to Non-Aristotelian Systems and General Semantics*. Third Edition. Lakeville, Connecticut: The International Non-Aristotelian Library Publishing Company, 1948.

_____. *Time-Binding: The General Theory*. Lakeville, Connecticut: The Institute of General Semantics, 1949.

Kraemer, Hendrik. *The Communication of the Christian Faith.* Philadelphia: The Westminster Press, 1956.

Laird, Charlton. *The Miracle of Language.* Cleveland and New York: The World Publishing Company, 1953.

Langer, Susanne K. *Philosophy in a New Key.* New York: The New American Library of World Literature, Inc. (Mentor Books), 1951.

Larrabee, Harold A. *Reliable Knowledge.* Boston: Houghton Mifflin Company, 1945.

Leach, William H. *Handbook of Church Management.* Englewood Cliffs, New Jersey: Prentice-Hall Inc., 1958.

Lee, Irving J. *Customs and Crises in Communication.* New York: Harper & Brothers, 1954.

——————. *How to Talk With People.* New York: Harper & Brothers, 1952.

——————. *Language Habits in Human Affairs.* New York: Harper & Brothers, 1941.

—————— (ed.). *The Language of Wisdom and Folly*: *Background Readings in General Semantics.* New York: Harper & Brothers, 1949.

——————, and Laura L. Lee. *Handling Barriers in Communication*: *Lectures-Discussions and Conferee's Handbook.* New York: Harper & Brothers, 1957.

Lewin, Kurt. *Field Theory in Social Science.* Editor Dorwin Cartwright. New York: Harper & Brothers, (Harper Torchbooks), 1951.

——————, and Ronald Lippitt. "An Experimental Approach to the Study of Autocracy and Democracy: A Preliminary Note," *Sociometry A Journal of Interpersonal Relations,* I (January-April, 1938), 292-300.

Lewis, H. D. (ed.). *Clarity is not Enough*: *Essays in Criticism of Linguistic Philosophy.* New York: Humanities Press, 1963.

Lindgren, Alvin J. *Foundations for a Purposeful Church*

Administration. New York: Abingdon Press, 1965.

Lippitt, Gordon L., and Edith Seashore. *The Leader and Group Effectiveness.* New York: Association Press, 1962.

Logan, Harlan, and Lawrence G. Blochman. *Are You Misunderstood?* New York: Wilfred Funk, Inc., 1965.

Longabaugh, Theodore. *General Semantics an Introduction.* New York, Washington, Hollywood, Toronto: Vantage Press, 1957.

Luccock, Halford E. *Communicating the Gospel.* New York: Harper & Brothers, 1954.

McDaniel, E. F. *Discovering the Real Self.* New York: Philosophical Library, 1958.

McLaughlin, Raymond W., "Intensional-Extensional Language As A Measure of Semantic Orientation," *Bulletin Of The Evangelical Theological Society,* X (Summer, 1967), 143-151.

McLuhan, Marshall, *The Gutenberg Galaxy The Making of Typographic Man.* University of Toronto Press, 1962.

----------------------, *The Mechanical Bride Folklore of Industrial Man.* New York: The Vanguard Press, Inc., 1951.

----------------------, *Understanding Media The Extensions Of Man.* New York, Toronto, London: McGraw-Hill Book Company, 1964.

Mascall, E. L. *Words and Images a Study in Theological Discourse.* London, New York, Toronto: Longmans, Green and Co., Inc., 1957.

Mead, George H. *Mind, Self and Society.* Chicago: The University of Chicago Press, 1934.

Miller, Paul M. *Group Dynamics in Evangelism.* Scottdale, Pennsylvania: Herald Press, 1958.

Minteer, Catherine. *Words and What They Do to You Beginning Lessons in General Semantics for Junior and Senior High School.* Evanston, Illinois, White Plains, New York: Row, Peterson and Company, 1953.

Moray, Neville. *Cybernetics.* New York: Hawthorn Books, Publishers, 1963.

Moreno, J. L. *Who Shall Survive? A New Approach to the Problem of Human Interrelations.* Collaborator: Helen H. Jennings. Washington: Nervous and Mental Diseases Publishing Company, 1934.

Morris, Charles W. *Signs, Language and Behavior.* New York: George Braziller, Inc., 1955.

Morrison, A. Cressy. *Man Does Not Stand Alone.* Westwood, New Jersey: Fleming Revell Company, 1944.

Murray, Elwood, Raymond H. Barnard, and J. V. Garland. *Integrative Speech.* New York: The Dryden Press, 1953.

----------------------------. *The Speech Personality.* Revised. Chicago, Philadelphia, and New York: J. B. Lippincott Company, 1944.

Nichols, Ralph G., and Leonard A. Stevens. *Are You Listening?* New York: McGraw-Hill Book Company, Inc., 1957.

----------------------------, and Thomas R. Lewis. *Listening and Speaking a Guide to Effective Oral Communication.* Dubuque, Iowa: Wm. C. Brown Company Publishers, 1954.

Nichols, Sue. *Words on Target: For Better Christian Communication.* Richmond, Virginia: John Knox Press, 1963.

Nida, Eugene A. *Message and Mission the Communication of the Christian Faith.* New York: Harper & Brothers, 1960.

Nygren, Anders. *Agape and Eros.* trans., Philip S. Watson. London: S. P. C. K., 1953.

Ogden, C. K., and I. A. Richards. *The Meaning of Meaning.* New York: Harcourt, Brace and Company, 1923.

Osborn, Alex F. *Creative Imagination.* New York: Scribners, 1957.

Osgood, Charles E., George J. Suci, and Percy Tannenbaum.

The Measurement of Meaning. Urbana, Illinois: The University of Illinois Press, 1957.

Overstreet, Harry and Bonaro. *The Mind Alive*. New York: W. W. Norton & Company, 1954.

Perry, Lloyd M., and Edward J. Lias. *A Manual of Pastoral Problems and Procedures*. Grand Rapids, Michigan: Baker Book House, 1962.

Ramsey, Ian T. *Religious Language*. London: SCM Press Ltd., 1957.

Rankin, Paul T. "The Importance of Listening Ability," *English Journal*, College Edition, XVII (October, 1928), 623-30.

Rapaport, Anatol. *Operational Philosophy*. New York: Harper & Brothers, 1953.

_____. *Science and the Goals of Man*. New York: Harper & Brothers, 1950.

Roethlisberger, F. J., and W. J. Dickson. *Management and the Worker*. Cambridge: Harvard University Press, 1939.

Rokeach, Milton. *The Open and Closed Mind*. New York: Basic Books, Inc., Publishers, 1960.

Ross, Murray, and Charles E. Hendry. *New Understanding of Leadership A Survey and Application of Research*. New York: Association Press, 1957.

Ruesch, Jurgen. *Disturbed Communication*. New York: W. W. Norton and Company, 1957.

_____, and Gregory Bateson. *Communication the Social Matrix of Psychiatry*. New York: W. W. Norton & Company, Inc., 1951.

_____, and Weldon Kees. *Nonverbal Communication*. Berkeley and Los Angeles: University of California Press, 1956.

Schramm, Wilbur (ed.). *The Process and Effects of Mass Communication*. Urbana, Illinois: The University of Illinois Press, 1954.

Sellers, R. W. *The Essentials of Logic.* Boston: Houghton Mifflin Company, 1945.

Shannon, Claude, and Warren Weaver. *The Mathematical Theory of Communication.* Urbana: The University of Illinois Press, 1949.

Shepherd, Clovis R. *Small Groups Some Sociological Perspectives.* San Francisco: Chandler Publishing Company, 1964.

Slavson, S. R. *An Introduction to Group Therapy.* New York: International Universities Press, 1943.

Sondell, Bess. *The Humanity of Words A Primer of Semantics.* Cleveland and New York: The World Publishing Company, 1958.

Sorokin, Pitirim A. *Explorations in Altruistic Love and Behavior.* Boston: Beacon Press, 1954.

------------------------------. *Forms and Techniques of Altruistic and Spiritual Growth.* Boston: Beacon Press, 1954.

------------------------------. *The Ways and Power of Love.* Boston: Beacon Press, 1954.

Stock, Dorothy, and Herbert A. Thelen. *Emotional Dynamics and Group Culture.* Washington: National Training Laboratories, 1958.

Thelen, Herbert A. *Dynamics of Groups at Work.* Chicago: The University of Chicago Press, 1954.

Thurman, Kelly (ed.). *Semantics.* Boston: Houghton Mifflin Company, 1960.

Urban, Wilbur Marshall. *Language and Reality the Philosophy of Language and the Principles of Symbolism.* London: George Allen & Unwin Ltd., New York: The Macmillan Company, 1951.

Watson, J. S. (trans.). *Cicero on Oratory and Orators.* Philadelphia: David McKay, Publishers, 1897.

Weinberg, Harry L. *Levels of Knowing and Existence.* New York: Harper & Brothers, 1957.

Weschler, Irving R. *The Leader and Creativity*. New York: Association Press, 1962.

Whatmough, Joshua. *Language A Modern Synthesis*. New York: The New American Library of World Literature, Inc., (Mentor Books), 1956.

Weiner, Norbert. *The Human Use of Human Beings*. Second edition revised. Garden City, New York: Doubleday & Company, Inc., 1954.

Wittenberg, Rudolph M. *The Art of Group Discipline*. New York: Association Press, 1951.

Woodworth, Hugh. *The Nature and Technique of Understanding: Some Fundamentals of Semantics*. Vancouver, B.C.: The Wrigley Printing Company Ltd., 1949.

Young, J. Z. *Doubt and Certainty in Science*. London: Oxford University Press, 1953.

Zipf, G. K. *The Psychobiology of Language*. Boston: Houghton Mifflin, 1935.

Subject Index

Abstraction process, 52 ff.
 — and self-reflexiveness, 55 ff.
 — chart of, 54
 —clarity, 54 f.
 — dead level, 55
Accent, 142 ff.
Action research, 191 f.
Ad hominem arguments, 132 ff.
Ad populum arguments, 135 ff.
Adjustment in intrapersonal communication, 65
Allness, 36, 100 ff.
 — and non-allness, 72
Amphiboly, 140 ff.
Analogy, false, 120 ff.
Annual report, 114 ff.
Arguing in circles, 127
Assuming the truth of a proposition, 129
Authority, 123 ff.
 — criteria of, 126
Authoritarian led group, 154
Average, What is? 111

Begging the question, 127 ff.
Brainstorming, 187
Buzz session, 187 f.

Cause and effect, invalid, 108 ff.
Change of sense data, 21 ff., 46 f.
Channels, 83 ff.
 — group, 85

 — mass, 84 f.
 — physical, 84
 — technical, 84
Character (*Ethos*) of the speaker, 71 ff.
Church
 — as a group, 150 ff.
 — definition of, 18
Clouding the issue, 139 ff.
Communicator, 71 ff.
 — appearance of, 74
 — attitudes of, 74
 — character of, 71 ff.
 — evaluations of, 77
 — knowledge of, 76
 — skills of, 78
Communication
 — and distortion of information, 24, 29
 — and moral and social evils, 23
 — and psychological problems, 22
 —barriers, 97 ff.
 — breakdown, 21
 — definition of, 17
 — group, 66 ff., 173 ff.
 — importance of, 19 f.
 — ingredients of, 69 f.
 — interpersonal, 62 ff.
 — intrapersonal, 62 ff.
 — levels of, 67
 — models of, 69 f.

224

Author Index

227